W9-CHV-901

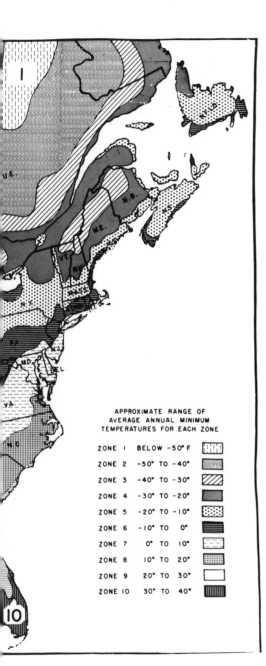

APPROXIMATE RANGE OF
AVERAGE ANNUAL MINIMUM
TEMPERATURES FOR EACH ZONE

ZONE 1	BELOW -50° F	
ZONE 2	-50° TO -40°	
ZONE 3	-40° TO -30°	
ZONE 4	-30° TO -20°	
ZONE 5	-20° TO -10°	
ZONE 6	-10° TO 0°	
ZONE 7	0° TO 10°	
ZONE 8	10° TO 20°	
ZONE 9	20° TO 30°	
ZONE 10	30° TO 40°	

The Zones of Plant Hardiness

This map, prepared by the U.S. Department of Agriculture, shows hardiness Zones 2 through 10, each representing an area of winter hardiness for plants. Of course, the zones do not represent hard-and-fast conditions; areas in adjacent zones must also be taken into consideration, as well as mini-climates and protected situations. The adaptability of a plant is also influenced by its location, within a zone, as to sunlight, rainfall, and soil composition, as well as zone temperatures. If allowances are made for these inevitable variations, planting by zone can be extremely helpful, a guide to winter flowers and color, and for some far northern plants a guide to their summer survival southward.

Color for Your Winter Yard & Garden

2 50

Books by Helen Van Pelt Wilson

A Garden in the House

House Plants for Every Window
(*with Dorothy H. Jenkins*)

The Complete Book of African Violets

The Joy of Flower Arranging

Climbing Roses

Roses for Pleasure (*with Richard Thomson*)

The New Perennials Preferred

Flower Arrangement Designs for Today (*Editor*)

The Joy of Geraniums

The Fragrant Year (*with Léonie Bell*)

African-violet and Gesneriad Questions
Answered by Twenty Experts (*Editor*)

1001 African-violet Questions
Answered by Twelve Experts (*Editor*)

Helen Van Pelt Wilson's African-violet Book

Flowers, Space, and Motion

Joyful Thoughts for Five Seasons (*anthology*)

Helen Van Pelt Wilson's Own
Garden and Landscape Book

House Plants Are for Pleasure

Successful Gardening in the Shade

Successful Gardening with Perennials

Color for Your Winter Yard and Garden

Color for Your Winter Yard & Garden

WITH FLOWERS, BERRIES, BIRDS, AND TREES

Helen Van Pelt Wilson

Charles Scribner's Sons
New York

Copyright © 1978 Helen Van Pelt Wilson

Library of Congress Cataloging in Publication Data

Wilson, Helen Van Pelt, 1901-
   Color for your winter yard and garden.

   Includes index.
   1. Winter gardening.   2. Color in gardening.
I. Title.
SB439.5.W54   635.9'53   77-13822
ISBN 0-684-15359-9

Two excerpts from this book appeared in
Flower & Garden, © 1977 by Helen Van Pelt Wilson.
One excerpt appeared in *Horticulture,* © 1978
by Massachusetts Horticultural Society.

This book published simultaneously in the
United States of America and in Canada —
Copyright under the Berne Convention

All rights reserved. No part of this book
may be reproduced in any form without the
permission of Charles Scribner's Sons.

1 3 5 7 9 11 13 15 17 19 MD/C 20 18 16 14 12 10 8 6 4 2

Printed in the United States of America

For
Helen B. Krieg
invaluable secretary, alert critic,
cherished friend

Contents

Charts

Planting Plans
by Eloise Ray, L.A.

Therefore all seasons shall be sweet to thee,
Whether the summer clothe the general earth
With greenness, or the redbreast sit and sing
Betwixt the tufts of snow on the bare branch
Of mossy apple-tree, while the night thatch
Smokes in the sun-thaw; whether the eave-drops fall
Heard only in the trances of the blast,
Or if the secret ministry of frost
Shall hang them up in silent icicles,
Quietly shining to the quiet Moon.

SAMUEL TAYLOR COLERIDGE

Some Thoughts on Winter

TODAY IS December 21, the first day of winter, according to the calendar, but the cold descended weeks ago and there was even a brief snow flurry this year in mid-November, only a hint of a possible blizzard to come. But even when the world is covered with snow and we see it mainly as a black-and-white print, there is also color.

And no winter color is more brilliant than that of the rising sun. I watch the gorgeous panorama from my breakfast table, the spectacle being late enough, in winter, for comfortable viewing. First, the whole east glows crimson. As this color deepens, the great globe of the sun rises majestically, the form bold and complete. It holds briefly, giving way quickly to a glowing orb of pure light that swiftly mounts the cold gray sky. Then the gray world turns blue, shadows lengthen, and streaks of light gleam through the openings in my picket fence. The short winter day ends before five o'clock as sunset stains the west with a rosy light like the color of dawn that earlier painted the east. Soon the rising full moon casts a shining light over my silent snow-covered world and night becomes almost as brilliant as day.

I enjoy the unique quality of winter. It is a season of short days and long thoughts. I have favorite poems to read again. Whittier's old-fashioned *Snow-Bound* gives me fresh pleasure. Snug by my fragrant apple-wood fire while the wind rages without, I delight again in the Quaker poet's "universe of sky and snow."

For me, this fourth season is full of peace and beauty. Yet consider the words hurled at it by less appreciative poets—sad, dreary, doleful, rude, dull, joyless, baleful, a time when "winds are wearily sighing." For me it is never dull, certainly never colorless. Hemlocks and hollies are a deep, living green; junipers are touched with bronze, blue-gray, even purple; birches gleam in any situation—so, too, do the white clusters of the snowberries, the brilliant red fruits of Washington thorn and the American cranberry bush. Late in January or in early February the aconites offer their golden cups.

Why do I love winter so? I am not quite sure why this serene season so stimulates me to meditation and philosophy. A perspicacious friend maintains that my feeling is due to release from the exhausting labors of other years when I coped with acreage. Now, with my smaller place, I have much less work to do. In any case, I appreciate the special aspects of the season—the cold, still, sparkling air; the night silence; the long hours of darkness; the slower tempo of life; and the brilliance of sunrise, moonlight, and starlight.

In summer the fine forms of deciduous trees are lost in their canopies of leaves; in summer we may not notice the different qualities of bark or the architectural balance of forms. Striking in winter are the spectacular pink-white flowers of Christmas roses that open by the terrace; and long before the end of winter, which is March 21, the myriad blooms of small bulbs—yellow crocuses, white snowdrops, purple irises, and tiny yellow narcissus—push through the thawing earth. Often, while patches of snow remain, they brighten my garden in this season that some poets dare to declare "dreary" or "drab." And at night, how the beauty of the garden is enhanced and the shadows lengthened by the soft light of my post lantern gleaming down upon the dwarf evergreens and green ground covers.

As for birds in winter, how noticeable are their colors at this time, particularly the blue jay and red cardinal, and the less vivid purple finch and red-breasted nuthatch. In winter they are amusing companions, and I can only suggest, to anyone who is lonely, that you invite the birds, and hours of exciting companionship will be yours. I know I can never read a book with any degree of concentration if I sit facing a window in view of the feeders here.

Of all seasons I love winter best, the beauty of the snow-covered landscape, the calm of the cold months. Spring is exciting; summer, languorous; fall, an exuberant triumph of color; but in my four-season garden, winter has a final clean-cut charm.

1977   Helen Van Pelt Wilson

About This Book

THE PURPOSE OF THIS BOOK is twofold: to open your eyes to the very special beauties of the winter scene, and to interest you in developing a four-season garden. The wisely planted place should give you just as beautiful, though different, pictures in winter as in the three other seasons.

The charts that follow the chapters are selective, not all-inclusive, for the possibilities of suitable winter material can be overwhelming. If I warn you about setting out trees that may become giants in twenty years, it is not because I do not appreciate great oaks and beeches, but because I hope to help you make the most of your place with a variety of smaller trees and shrubs. With bulbs and perennials, these can provide a long panorama of color. Of course, if you have a great specimen tree on your property, enjoy to the full its changing beauty through the year.

As time—and strength—have permitted, I have followed here the nomenclature of *Hortus Third*.* My own text was completed before the publication of that book, and the plant names were then consistent with former usage. However, because of both my respect for the work of the staff of the Liberty Hyde Bailey Hortorium in bringing *Hortus Second* up to date and the need of horticultural writers to have one final authority for plant names, I have now made the names and their typographic styling conform to those in *Hortus Third*.

*Hortus Third: A Dictionary of Plants Cultivated in the United States and Canada, by the staff of the L. H. Bailey Hortorium, Cornell University. New York: Macmillan, Inc., 1976.

The "Zone" column in each chart indicates the north-south range in which any listed species will thrive with suitable soil and moisture. Bear in mind that there are local variations within each zone depending upon altitude, average rainfall, prevailing winds, and proximity to the sea. Some northern plants—notably most spruces, some species of pine, willow, birch, and others—cannot endure the warm summers of the lower South or the dry summers of the Middle West.

To help you plan the best possible winter effects, determine your own zone according to the endpaper map, which indicates each locality and the temperatures you may expect.

The dates of bloom in this book have been based, of course, on many winters before 1977. This year our windows looked out on quite different scenes from those of earlier years—snowdrifts, snow-draped hemlocks, ice-encased maples. In January no winter aconites opened their yellow flowers; in February no wintersweet, no crocuses, not even snowdrops bloomed. The Christmas roses, whose white stems were already in evidence last November, did not produce flowers until February. For me it was a beautiful winter, but my work keeps me indoors with no commuting, so my fenced-in garden gave me great pleasure—the little standard lilacs etched against the snow, the birds enjoying my bounty at the kitchen window. Of course, I hope my records of early flowers will be repeated in future years. Meanwhile I admire and enjoy winter as she presents herself.

Color for Your Winter Yard & Garden

From my living-room window, a small ceramic squirrel perched on a log, in a grove of mountain laurel, birch, viburnum, and pachysandra, always delights me. *Swinehart photo*

1

What Do *You* See from Your Winter Windows?

You don't have to go outdoors to enjoy a colorful winter garden. In fact, it is good landscaping to lay out your garden so that it offers pleasing pictures from the windows of the rooms you use most. The modern trend in home building toward more and larger windows, sometimes whole walls of glass, emphasizes the point. Winter window views of your garden become most effective when you select interesting plants and then arrange them to play up contrasts of light and dark, the components of structure and pattern, with the tang of color accents against a bold, or at least definite, background.

In every winter garden well-placed evergreens and fruiting shrubs are pace-makers. These are best placed prominently opposite a dining-room, living-room, or perhaps landing window, a likely place at which to pause and look through the indoor vines to the outdoor scene. And through the windows how bright are the cold-weather bits of crimson, purple, or white that the shrubs supply! Sparkling as a blue jay in a snow flurry, they stand out in the quiescent beauty of winter.

For key spots important all through winter, there is a long and tempting list of shrubs and small trees to be considered. If these are deciduous, they will be all the handsomer with a firm background of pine or hemlock to silhouette their

From my former study window I enjoyed a country view of a snow-covered hill with a rock ledge. *Krieg Photo*

forms and emphasize the brightness of their winter buds or fruits. As Gertrude Jekyll has noted, "The winter garden is all the better for the fewness of its flowers. The summer garden is only too full of brilliant objects of beauty and interest, and the winter garden should have its own rather contrasting character as a place of comparative repose of mind and eye."

If you are planning a new garden, give special thought to an interesting design that will be particularly pleasing in winter, when there is less distraction of trees in leaf and flowers in bloom. If the present winter view from the windows over-looking your already planted place is hardly a view at all but only an indifferent mixture of leafless trees and formless evergreens (maybe your neighbor's trash as well), you can remedy this without superhuman effort. You can, for example, set out a few groups of evergreens of varying shades of green, along with one handsome deciduous tree and red- or white-berried shrubs in front of it, situating these plantings perhaps along the far boundaries of your place. Or you can add

ABOVE: On a snowy day this view of my small fenced-in garden (where nothing needs doing) gives me quiet pleasure. *Fitch photo*

RIGHT: Snow on dark green hemlocks with the contrasting forms of a leaf-less birch tree and viburnums is a picture I enjoy looking down upon from my bedroom above. *Swinehart photo*

certain shrubs to otherwise ineffective plantings and so develop associations far more interesting than the haphazard specimens that have so far counted for little. The planting plans in Chapter 8 may suggest ideas for your place.

In any case, to ensure winter survival of the plants you select, check your zone on the map in the endpapers. If you live in a zone farther north than that indicated in the charts in this book, Zone 3 for instance, your plants will not be likely to survive the winter. If you live south of the zones indicated, you cannot enjoy some of the far northern plants, such as certain junipers and viburnums. They will not do well in the parts of Zones 8 and 9 where winters are too warm and humid or summers too hot and dry.

In addition to trees and shrubs, select some of the flowering plants that bloom delightfully in cold weather, and situate them close to the house. Right next to the warming walls of chimney and house, set the winter-blooming hellebores (the Christmas roses are the first of these to open) and the very early hardy bulbs. Plan also, with special feeders, to attract the birds that usually do not migrate—the cardinal, blue jay, purple finch, titmouse, junco, chickadee—and the various northern species that occasionally surprise us—grosbeaks, fox sparrows, kinglets, and the mysterious snowy owl.

Sculpture for the Garden

Have you considered the pleasure a well-placed piece of garden sculpture can give you in winter? In a setting all its own—like my small squirrel in its grove of hemlock, birch, and pachysandra—it will delight you. However, when you select sculpture for prominent placement outside a window, be sure the piece is weatherproof. Wood and marble are not weather-resistant materials, nor is terra cotta, unless the surface is sealed against moisture with a heavy coat of clear outdoor shellac. (My own much-prized pair of ceramic doves is stored in the cellar.) Copper sculptures turn a pleasing blue-green, and hammered lead offers no problems; iron needs occasional light oiling and protection from rust, so I would not select this material. And incidentally, I would avoid subjects such as naked cherubs, charming as they are in summer. In winter I want to offer them a coat or shawl.

Particularly suited to the garden are sculptures of natural association—birds, squirrels (unless these are anathema to you because of their destructive tenden-

A Saint Francis figure, silhouetted against a brown fence and in a setting of rhododendron and pachysandra with a drift of foreground snow, makes a serene garden picture to dwell upon with pleasure from living-room windows. *Taloumis photo*

cies, though I do enjoy their winter frolics), a griffin, even a sphinx. Perhaps you would like a Saint Francis with a birdbath at his feet. A friend has such a piece which she found in a shop specializing in garden sculpture. The finished pieces there were terribly expensive and she was about to give up the whole idea when she spied on a shelf some small, appealing figures of Saint Francis that were cast in plaster, which she was told could not be guaranteed to withstand the rigors of winter. However, she secured one of these for about ten dollars and gave it a heavy coat of weather-resistant gray paint, and when this was dry, she applied a thin coat of outdoor green paint, the color of weathered copper. While the green paint was still wet, she lightly wiped the high parts of the molded figure with a soft cloth to let a little of the gray beneath show through. This gave a stronger effect of light and shade as well as the weathered look desired. The little figure has withstood more than twenty winters with no damage and with new paint applied only once. This paint method could also be used to tone down the new and shiny appearance of an inexpensive plastic figure of the type so often sold at roadside stands.

If you are seeking a piece of sculpture, you might find it at the shop of a local artist or possibly at an exhibition of sculpture in your area. If you live near

In this green winter garden of euonymus, andromeda, dwarf rhododendron 'Dora Amateius', mugho pine, and yews, a unicorn figure makes an effective accent at the end of a flagstone path. Connecticut garden of Mr. and Mrs. Orville Prescott. *Owner photo*

New York City, do visit The Florentine Craftsmen, Inc., 654 First Avenue. There you will see a fine display of animal and figure pieces, handsome sundials too, perhaps just what you want, and the prices are not exorbitant.

I hope none of your garden requires burlap swathing as protection against wind and cold. For every geographic area there are plants suited to the climate, and these are the best choice. I know how dear to many are paths bordered with English boxwood, but when protected with burlap these are far from attractive in winter. Better to plant a border of American box or upright yew or Korean box that will readily survive your winters. There are nearly always good climatic substitutes of the right shape. I once had a little rose tree that required bundling up at the top. This made it unsightly all winter while a pair of standard lilacs, *Syringa palibiniana*, of the same form and 40-inch height proved winterproof without any covering.

The birches are the only plants to receive special winter attention in my geographic area, Zone 6. With a broom I sweep off any snow burden that bends them down and interferes with the intricate moving shadows made by their graceful branches. If you have evergreens that bend dangerously under the weight of snow, apply a broom to them as well, and do this early, before the snow turns to ice and causes severe breakage.

The Neat Look with Winter Mulches

A place properly prepared for winter is indeed a pleasant sight. "Leave the garden in the fall the way you want to find it in the spring" is wise advice; and so the grass is mowed well into November, if it is still growing then, and the driveway and the walk are sharply edged, unless, of course, plants of myrtle or hardy candytuft flow over gently as they do here. *Where it is needed*, a winter mulch evenly applied *after* a frozen crust forms on the ground is a necessary safety measure. Its purpose is to keep the cold in and so avoid the dangers of alternate freezing and thawing. Persistent snow gives natural protection but that cannot be counted on in most states.

Don't provide cold-weather protection unless it is needed; overheating plants can be fatal. If your garden has hedge or wall protection, a winter mulch may be unnecessary, and that is nice, for applying a mulch in fall and then removing it in spring is a great bother. For some years I have not used any coverings here in

Zone 6. Of course, I am near Long Island Sound, and nearness to water always mitigates cold. Furthermore, my small garden is protected by a picket fence and I grow few "difficult" plants. Unless the area is very cold, peonies, iris, Oriental poppies, and delphinium require no covering except in the first winter after planting. Day lilies never need protection.

You can find or produce good mulching materials right on your own place. Leaves are a mulch that collects naturally. They catch among the crowns of the plants in the perennial border (the tall tops are, of course, cut down before mulching). But more leaves usually have to be added to get uniform distribution. Any leaves will do except those of the poplars and Norway maples, which mat down like soggy rags and exclude all air from the plants while pressing down upon them all winter long. Leaves of oak, birch, hickory, beech, linden, and the harder wooded maples, such as the sugar maple, are fine. Indeed, any leaves that curl when they fall will do, while those that lie flat will not.

Leaves may be collected in baskets or piled in a corner of the yard until needed in mid-December, or later if a hard freeze has not occurred by that time. Then they are spread neatly over the ground, and a few evergreen boughs, perhaps lopped-off Christmas-tree branches, are arranged on top to hold them in place.

If you maintain a compost heap, you have the best possible mulching material at hand. The fine crumbly leaves spread 2 inches deep protect in winter and, worked into the soil in spring, are richly nutritious. If you have a stand of pine trees, gather the fallen needles and spread them 2 to 3 inches deep over the beds; they look fine. Or you can buy mulching material. Salt hay makes an excellent well-aerated mulch. It can be purchased by the bale and used for more than one winter, although between seasons it must be stored where it is not a fire hazard. Wood chips sold by town-maintenance crews and tree-pruning firms make attractive 2-inch mulches. But my favorites are redwood or pine-bark nuggets spread an inch or so deep. They come in several sizes and break down slowly. Since I cover my beds with these in summer just for looks, I add just enough in fall for even coverage.

With plants that maintain green tops throughout winter—foxglove, hollyhock, primrose, and Madonna lily—coverings are drawn under, not over, the tops. For these, and for woolly-leaved subjects like mulleins, a layer of small stones does the job well. In *Winterize Your Yard and Garden* (Philadelphia and New York: J. B. Lippincott Company) my friend George Taloumis describes a number of other safety procedures for plants subject to severe damage in northern areas.

What to Do If You Have Messy Neighbors

Too often it seems that those of us who care most about our yards and gardens have neighbors who care least. So the winter view at the sides and back of our properties can be particularly depressing. With concealing foliage gone (the leaves often left in piles in a halfhearted cleanup), the careless mess is even more unpleasant. Those of us who have suffered the winter look of children's broken toys—or a long-discarded wading pool now overturned and white-bright as the North Star, or rusted barbecue stands, or the leaning poles of a short-interest vegetable garden—have discovered certain, though hardly infallible, panaceas. Perhaps one of these will help you as they have me in my new location with adjacent neighbors. (When I lived in Stony Brook Cottage, no such problems confronted me because my neighbors were comfortably distant, with New England walls or woodland between us.)

A landscape gardener gave me an excellent idea, the best one of all, I think. "Don't try to cut off the view at a distance," she told me; "plan something close at hand that will *block* your view or hold your attention at, say, 10 to 15 feet from your house." A specimen white pine set outside my fence has proved a miracle of concealment of a neighbor's trash heap. A tall juniper of some density would do as well, or a dwarf pine or spruce with a rock in front or behind it, or a fine deciduous azalea placed to silhouette a rock, or a shapely rock set alone. A piece of garden statuary, even an interesting section of gnarled wood, could be propitiously placed instead of a rock. Such arrangements will not only block your neighbor's outrages but will provide you with delightful winter pictures. Or you might plant a handsome weeping tree. This worked delightfully for a couple who occupied a town house in a condominium. The property strip was narrow and the view beyond hardly engaging, so they set out an 8-foot weeping crab apple about 15 feet from the big window opposite their dining table. In all seasons this small tree was a delight, shapely in winter, flower-covered in spring, and a view-stopper of obvious value.

High fences along your property line—if these are locally permitted—make beautiful barriers when planted with vines such as the evergreen winter creeper *Euonymus fortunei*, or the fast-growing pyracantha. Solid split-cedar or stockade

A shapely deciduous azalea in a setting of rocks and snow arrests the attention, and in certain situations something similar might be planted to block an undesirable view beyond. *Swinehart photo (Oliver Nurseries, Fairfield, Conn.)*

fencing, available in 8-foot sections and 4- to 8-foot heights, can be concealing and also quite "gardenesque" barriers. A friend in an unpleasing neighborhood enclosed her entire property with this fencing and it gave her place the air of a private park. Where boundary space permitted, she "lined" the fence with American arborvitae, and where a neighbor's unsightly greenhouse with dirty summer glass demanded attention from her front door, she planted one tall Japanese cryptomeria.

In tight neighborhoods, boundary fences or plantings are trustworthy providers of privacy and good views. Hedges of quick-growing privet, pruned only to shapeliness the first few years, make nice green baffles quite quickly, and the plants are inexpensive. Long thick plantings of deciduous shrubs can be enjoyed in winter and are a source of flowers later. Evergreen hedges are most attractive —also more costly, but they do more. Arborvitaes planted 2 feet apart will do the trick, but their winter here is definitely rusty. Hemlocks keep their true green and are my favorites.

Following the boundary plan, I planted a row of 3-foot hemlocks next to an ill-kept church property. Well cared for, and I saw to that, the hemlocks grew some 18 inches a year and reached 7 feet at the end of the third summer. I had them topped a little then to thicken them and promote a more dense concealment. Every spring I dosed each tree generously with Holly-tone fertilizer, and in dry periods (I didn't wait for drought) I gave each tree a one- to two-hour soaking with a slow-running hose that reached from my faucet. Hemlocks have small root systems and are notably sensitive to dryness; they make a very handsome hedge, I think.

Probably the most insensitive neighbors are those who are sports-conscious. Golf, tennis, and boating occupy them, and they do not keep up a nice property. The most they are likely to do is mow their indifferent lawns occasionally, maybe every other week; their leaf-raking, started unenthusiastically in fall, is never quite finished so that only the welcome snow conceals the leaf piles left on their untidy places.

A friend who cares greatly about her new garden and the open stretch of property beyond solved this problem with consummate tact. Because she was inclined to overplant and her shubbery honestly *did* get overcrowded by the third year, she asked for, and obtained, permission from her neighbor to plant her extras in a long bed in their back yard, which was in her direct view and along their common boundary. At the corner she set out a young weeping willow, followed by a row of fast-growing *Viburnum tomentosum* (plus a few extra shrubs she bought). In two years the viburnums became an excellent barrier, even in winter after their leaves fell. She assumed the upkeep of the section she planted in her neighbor's yard, watering the bed frequently at the start with a hose section from her own faucet, and mulching the area deeply with big pine-bark nuggets.

Of course, your neighbors may not be so cooperative; they may view any such suggestion on your part as intrusion of their privacy—which undoubtedly it is, no matter how unattractive their privacy may be. If such a situation is your unhappy lot, you had better resort to view-stopping with some device of plant, stone, driftwood, or statuary set off by a natural background, all on your own property.

A couple whose property was their pride were greatly annoyed by their neighbor's driveway, which ran parallel to theirs and was only a few feet away. Here the children dropped soft-drink cans, papers, and other items; rubbish accumulated without disturbing the parents in the least. What to do? The couple's solution is simply to clean up their neighbor's driveway when they rake their

Inviting contemplation in any season, this 12-by-18-foot Zen garden is particularly pleasing in winter—the white-gravel rectangle framed with lava rock slabs and river stones, symbolizing man, earth, and heaven; the gravel swept to symbolize clouds. *Fitch photo (Hammond Museum, North Salem, N.Y.)*

own. Apparently this is managed with no hard feelings, the favor never acknowledged, the improvement quite unnoticed.

One meticulous lady was greatly comforted by her visiting grandson's quick cleanup of a neighbor's most objectionable summer leftovers. When the coast was clear, he tore over, picked up newspapers, hid a broken red chair under a pile of leaves, restructured the picnic table and benches that were scattered about, and placed a bright-green watering can and a yellow pail on the neighbor's steps. He returned breathless but triumphant, and there was no unpleasant aftermath from next door. Could be the neighbors never knew the difference!

Perhaps you who despair over the dismal sights you see through your winter windows can find a panacea here. Maybe you will come up with a new plan once you put your mind to it. Anyway, your problem is rarely insoluble and a pleasant

Seen from my kitchen window, this black-and-white vignette of a young viburnum is pretty as an etching. *Swinehart photo*

winter view is worth achieving even if it requires considerable effort and some expense.

Plants for the Cold Season

Even limited areas like my own small plots can include some winter plants of significance. Today a number of dwarf evergreens are available, like the dwarf yew, false cypress, and Alberta spruce that I enjoy. Also in my garden are two leucothoe and an andromeda, euonymus vines on the divider and fence, English ivy on a small stretch of wall, a strip of evergreen Christmas ferns, various evergreen hellebores, a big winter honeysuckle shrub—*Lonicera fragrantissima* —outlining myrtle and hardy candytuft, and a patch of epimedium, though this turns brown. These contribute to my winter scene and accent the balanced design; so does the delicate tracery of some small shrub like a newly planted viburnum.

Your winter garden can also please *you* with every glance through the windows of your hearth-warmed house to the cold-weather drama of evergreens, flowering and fruiting trees and shrubs, and even perennials and bulbs in full bloom—

In this four-season garden, winter presents a colorful picture with evergreens of different hues and a great clump of bronze azaleas under the spreading branches of a dogwood tree. A griffin presides on the gate post. On the right, a bird-feeder is set close to the house for easy watching and tending. Connecticut garden of Mr. and Mrs. Orville Prescott. *Owner photo*

a beautiful scene by day and under night lighting wonderfully exciting. It can be as rewarding, perhaps more so, than your summer garden, which makes such constant demands on your energies. It's all a matter of selection; so let us now consider colorful plants for winter, the fourth season, with its different but many delightful possibilities.

The Christmas rose, *Helleborus niger*, in long-lasting bloom despite the snow, makes a lovely winter picture, the white-to-rose flowers framed in evergreen leaves. *Roche photo*

2

Christmas Roses and
Other Winter Flowers

IF YOU PLAN YOUR GARDEN for four seasons instead of the usual three, in most climates you can have flowers even in winter. Besides the very early small bulbs (described in the next chapter), a number of perennials, strategically placed in warm, protected locations, will bloom as the snow melts. January may not be as floriferous as June, but it certainly can offer you considerable color. Let the hellebores be your first consideration.

Beautiful, exciting, free-blooming in the midst of snow is the Christmas rose, *Helleborus niger.* No summer plant can bring you more delight than this hellebore that comes into full flower in the depths of winter. Of course, it isn't a rose at all but a member of the large buttercup family, which includes the anemone, the columbine, the delphinium, and the peony. If the numerous hellebore species were available to us here (as I hope in time they will be and as they are now in England), our winter gardens could be adorned with a greater variety of their flower and plant forms. But if you have a number of mature plants of the Christmas rose alone, or just three as I have in one place, your cold-weather gardens can be bright indeed, for the porcelain beauty of each open flower makes a mature plant unbelievably lovely, and like no other in the temperate zones.

17

Two plants of *Helleborus niger* 'Altifolius'—recently moved to my new garden and sheltered by terrace wall, house wall, and step—bloom exuberantly for months in winter, the flowers protected from splashing of rain and snow by a mulch of wood chips and plants of ivy and myrtle. *Bukovcik photo*

The Hellebores

Helleborus niger comes from Europe, and March travelers in cold Austria and northern Italy are charmed there by the contrast of snow and blooms. One visitor wrote me: "We were driving from Salzburg to Bad Ischl and then to Bad Aussee and there was still much snow to be seen as we drove over mountain passes. When we reached the summit of the Potschen Pass (altitude 3,244 feet), we could see the Christmas roses, or *Schneerosen* as they are called in Austria, poking their heads through the snow. It was a beautiful day with the sun sparkling on the snow, and in one place, there were children along the roadside offering bunches of hellebores to passing motorists." Other travelers tell how astonished they were to find hellebores in mid-March in full bloom beside the steps of Austrian castles, and Italian visitors report that the plants grow especially well in the subalpine woods above Lake Como and Lake Garda.

The great plant explorer Reginald Farrer described the Christmas rose as "one of the candours of the world, in all its forms of a white and unchangeable flawlessness . . . *Helleborus niger*, so called because its heart or root is black while its face shines with a blazing white innocence."

The explorer's enthusiasm for this 12- to 15-inch plant is in no way exaggerated. In a protected corner of my garden, my oldest, most mature *H. n.* 'Altifolius' specimens, a taller, larger variety of the species, open their first pearly white buds late in January or February and in due course produce more than forty almost 5-inch-wide flowers. One year fat, white buds were visible at ground level on November 23. The flowers hold their perfection for months, finally turning deep rose. I cut off the leafless flower stems low down in late April or early May, leaving just a few to get dry and drop their seeds in an irregular circle around the parent plant. Meanwhile the handsome five-parted leaves that appear evergreen in winter get shabby as fresh new foliage pushes through. As this develops, I cut off the old leaves to give the fresh new ones space to expand.

Here a few other, if less spectacular but to me fascinating, hellebores flourish. The green-flowered British native *H. foetidus* opens its green buds about mid-January, and flowering continues well into March. Of this plant with its nine- to eleven-part leaves V. Sackville-West writes, "I like green flowers as those of *Helleborus foetidus*, the Setterwort, even more commonly and certainly more rudely called the stinking hellebore . . . I like any plant that will surprise me out of doors with flowers in January or February." Incidentally, there is no smell to the foetidus plant and only a slight unpleasantness to the root when it is broken.

In my garden this setterwort grows stiffly upright in front of fountainous plants of day lilies. The nodding green flowers, purple-tipped, appear on 2-foot stems above 12-inch mounds of ferny evergreen foliage. Several stems spring from each crown of a well-established plant, giving the effect of a small shrub. On this account, foetidus is a good companion for rhododendrons and azaleas and looks nice as an edging for other tall evergreens.

Another green hellebore that I read about in English books and long for is also a British native, the 2-foot *H. viridis*, whose foliage dies away in autumn, but I have been unable to locate it in this country. I believe I now have all species that are available here and the count is only five.

The Corsican hellebore, *H. lividus corsicus*, also flourishes for me in a bed with a day-lily background and produces bright green flowers on 2-foot stems above hollylike leaves, a nice possibility for Saint Patrick's Day bouquets. This too was a favorite of V. Sackville-West, who described it as "so strong and stout that its leaves alone have an architectural quality in the same sense as the Acanthus has an architectural or sculptural quality, quite apart from the beauty and value of the flowers." This one has three leaflets and is also the delight of winter-garden enthusiasts like the English writer M. J. Jefferson Brown, who has said of *H. corsicus*, "Some plants are spectacular for a month and nondescript for eleven. Other plants look well at all times. It is the hallmark of good breeding."

A hybrid, the so-called *H. X sternii,* in my garden looks very like the corsicus plants there except that the three-lobed foliage is a lighter, yellower green. The plant came to me in May with one small green-cupped flower. It continued to bloom, producing two more in July that lasted all summer. Whether this is a candidate for the winter garden, I do not know yet. However, it does belong with any collection of available hellebores, which is too limited as it is.

The showy 2- to 3-inch flowers of the Lenten rose, *H. orientalis* from Asia Minor, are not for winter. They open later, usually around Easter, and so do not belong in this winter discussion except to complete my hellebore story.

Considering my own pleasure and interest in hellebores, and my own proselytizing of them, I read with amusement Peter Coats's remark: "Hellebores, however they are named, are more popular with discerning gardeners today than they have ever been before. To have several varieties of hellebores in your garden is the sign of maturity of taste, of garden one-upmanship; they have become, in the gardening fraternity, a status symbol."

One thing is certain, hellebores are not for the gardener who wants quick results. You have to have patience, for most of the specimens we can buy are likely to be fairly small, with little possibility of bloom the first or second year after planting. To encourage the young plants that come to me in spring, I water them regularly, almost daily through the summer, depending of course on rainfall, and I apply a liquid fertilizer about once a week. With this attention, new leaves appear on young plants. Adult plants do not need this summer encouragement. Try to obtain the "extra large" clumps sometimes offered by growers.

Culture of Hellebores

Before setting buds, hellebores require not only maturity but comfort in their new locations, and they need to stay there, so select new homes with a view to permanency. Hellebores, like other winter-flowering plants, should be placed in a protected place—next to a chimney or house wall, beside steps, or in front of a protective barrier of evergreens, but always out of north and west winds. The more protected their location, the earlier they are likely to bloom. Although shade is usually recommended, my own good experience is based on providing sites that receive sun in winter and light, open shade—as under deciduous trees—in summer. A cool, moist location is ideal, and deep watering is essential in periods of drought. The soil that produces good flowering plants in your garden will usually suit the hellebores. However, since they are to stay put, it is a good idea to improve your average garden soil with plenty of compost or leaf mold, and to add sand until the soil feels coarse and light but is reliably moisture-retentive. (Here, the county soil test indicates extreme acidity in the hellebore bed and I am advised to add lime. I do not intend to do so as long as the plants are flourishing. In England the hellebores thrive in extremely sweet soils.)

I mulch my plants with compost and a light top layer of small wood chips for garden good looks. In any case, the hellebore bed must be deeply prepared. Take a look at those long, perpendicular roots and you will see why. (Incidentally, as far as my friends and I have discovered, hellebores do not take to pot culture; my thought is that pots are not formed to accommodate such deep roots.)

Set out plants in spring or in late August or September. In Zone 4 hellebores should be planted as early in fall as you can get them, so that they can have time to form new roots before the first frost arrives. Let the roots stretch down, not out. In a well-worked garden bed I prepare a 16-inch-deep hole for each plant, spacing the plants 15 inches apart, and setting the crowns just below the soil surface. Good drainage is essential; the fleshy roots will not survive dampness.

Frequent division is to be avoided. Not until the slow-growing plant has reached the ten- to twelve-leaf stage is separation worthwhile—and not really then, unless you are eager for more plants. The bigger the plants are, the more bountiful the bloom, even though it may seem to you that there is not enough room for the flower stems to push through the crowded crown.

As for pest and disease, my experience would indicate that these hellebores rarely get anything. I hear complaints of aphids but can't imagine their attacking these tough plants. I hear also of slugs. However, in my slug-ridden garden, where the battle never ceases and protection is assured, I have not seen slugs even *near* the hellebores. Occasionally a yellow leaf develops early in fall and I cut it off. In Washington, D.C., there are reports of poor performance, especially root trouble. I would guess the problem to be poor drainage, or a reaction to the high humidity there, which hellebores resent. In a word, then, once properly located and planted, hellebores are easy plants. Keep them well fed. I fertilize them in spring along with my other perennials, and again early in fall, since their flowering period is winter—December to May—not spring to fall like most other garden plants.

From Seed

Hellebores from seed are a slow business and almost impossible from commercial seed. Seed must be absolutely fresh for sowing with no journey between gathering and planting. Cold weather is essential for germination and there seems to be no use trying to fool the seeds into germination with a spell in the refrigerator. The best results come from seed gathered from your own or a neighbor's plant and sown immediately.

In spring cut back the "evergreen" foliage of winter as it disintegrates, while fine new light green leaf clusters thrust up through the center of the plants. The faded flowers now bend low to perfect and drop their seeds. For the sake of looks in my small garden, I cut off most of the blooms at the ground line, letting only a few remain. The soil below these is then not disturbed. Early the next spring, after the necessary freezing period of winter, germination will have occurred and tiny plants showing seed leaves will appear. By summer, true leaves will have developed and the small hellebores can then be safely transplanted. But they are far from flowering size; in fact, bloom should not be expected for two years or more. However, your rather expensive original plants will now have earned their keep.

Many of my best plants have come from Lamb Nurseries (E. 101 Sharp Ave., Spokane, Wash. 99202), so I queried them about their method of raising hellebores from seed. Here is their reply:

"We have found that they, like dictamnus and some other hard-shelled perennial seed, must be picked as soon as ripe and sown promptly. Cover the outdoor bed in a shady situation with about ¼-inch of clean sand and spread a piece of burlap or similar material over the sowing to conserve moisture. Keep the planting continuously damp; seed should germinate the following spring. We have had good results with our own fresh seed, but commercial seeds have usually dried too much and generally will not germinate until the second year, if at all. Seedlings emerge quite early in the spring, and they must be watched so that they do not get too rank before the burlap is removed. The seedlings are now ready to be separated and planted about 6 inches apart in a bed of fairly light soil."

For Bouquets

It's fun to put on outdoor cold-weather clothes to gather garden flowers in winter, and hellebores are well worth the trip. Friends who stop by for a flower or two report the bouquets stay fresh in water for ten days without special treatment. I always split the stems, as I do those of other heavy-stemmed flowers, resulting in a ten- or twelve-day length of house beauty that is a delight. At the end of that time, I have even revived a wilted spray for another good week by recutting the stems, steeping these for five minutes in a cup of boiling water, and then plunging them in a tall vase of ice water.

When you cut your bouquets, it's a good idea not to sacrifice hellebore foliage. Instead take sprays of English ivy, or pieces of pachysandra or other evergreens, to go with the flowers.

Growing hellebores can be a new experience and is almost inevitably rewarding. Do try them. Start with the Christmas rose. Perhaps it will bloom for you as early as December . . . as it hasn't yet for me. I hear reports of December flowers in Boston (Zone 5). In any case, you will enjoy blooms in later winter months and so extend your garden pleasure. You will find Christmas ferns and laurel good associates for Christmas roses; the heaths that are described in Chapter 4 and the very early bulbs of Chapter 3 are also wonderful companions.

Good Effects with Hellebores

Hellebores have excellent landscape possibilities that are almost unknown by most gardeners but a delight once they are discovered. A friend of mine in southern Pennsylvania parlayed one plant to fifteen in the course of about twelve years. Spread out under an ancient oak tree, with the protecting wall of an old springhouse for background, these hellebores made a surprising winter picture, one that began well before Christmas in most years. The lively white-to-rose profusion of flowers, with buds opening well into January, continued to be attractive into late March.

If you have a wide-spreading deciduous tree with deep, not surface, roots—an apple, oak, sweet gum, or ash perhaps—you can develop such a lovely winter scene. To accomplish this more quickly than my patient friend did, buy some well-developed plants for a start and divide these in due course.

Blooming on my entrance terrace in the dead of winter, hellebores not only astound but charm passersby, visitors, neighbors, and, of course, me. I have planted them to the fore of azaleas and evergreens that like the same somewhat acid soil conditions and with colonies of golden winter aconites in between.

You might enjoy hellebores as edging for one of *your* winter pictures. Perhaps your composition will include a tall hemlock that silhouettes a white birch, with white snowberries in front. Or, in a favored spot, you might place an American cranberry bush, a spreading native shrub with glowing red berries that persist through winter. A wide planting of white-flowering hellebores with this would be stunning. With either grouping you would see something quite special through your living-room windows in cold winter weather.

More Flowers for March

In addition to the hellebores, a few other perennials offer colorful bloom in cold climates. In favored locations, the first warm spell near the end of winter entices them to break through the thawing soil. A mixture of the feathery-foliaged Amur adonis, or Pheasant's-eye, *Adonis amurensis*, includes 2- to 3-inch flowers of pink, copper, orange, yellow, and white and stays colorful for almost two months. The spring adonis, *A. vernalis*, with yellow or white flowers, shows up a couple of weeks later but usually still blooms under the winter wire of March 21. Woods soil suits these plants, which thrive in sun or shade and reach a height of 15 inches in Zones 3 to 7. Sow commercial seeds in early fall or from your own plants before they disappear after bloom. The variety with double flowers, although grown by many gardeners, is sterile. A low-growing ground cover like sweet woodruff hides the disappearance of adonises and marks their location. Patches of snowdrops or blue scillas are pretty companions; a brilliant complement is the lilac-to-purple *Crocus sieberi*.

Louise Beebe Wilder was especially fond of *A. amurensis* and describes its allure this way: "With incredible speed there is thrust up the stout stalk, holding a foot in air its great suns of green-gold light. Nothing is so exciting at this time of year as this plant which is so little seen."

Nodding clusters of white, pink, or purple flowers rise just above rounded, sometimes evergreen leaves on 12-inch plants of the Himalayan *Bergenia ciliata (ligulata)*, the earliest of the bergenias to bloom. Suited to Zones 3 to 8, they prefer a moist, partially shaded spot and are charming there with a background of an evergreen fern, such as the common polypody or the maidenhair spleenwort, or beside a stretch of trout lily, which also likes dampness and often blooms late in March.

Also from the Himalayas, and preceding the more familiar vernal primroses, is the very hardy mid-March *Primula denticulata*, which grows to a height of 10 inches and may bloom right after snow melts. Flowers are soft lilac in color, or white in the variety 'Alba'; hybrids come in red, or in tints of pink or tones of purple. A semishaded, slightly sloped bed—as in a somewhat damp, humusy rock garden—is ideal. Good winter drainage is essential. Winter sun in March followed by the light shade of a burgeoning deciduous tree is another good location. Plants are divided when flowering is over. Doretta Klaber, an expert on primulas, made this pleasant comment:

"With the first breath of warm weather in March, the denticulatas thrust up small crisp leaves from the fat pink buds resting at the surface of the ground. Almost instantaneously, the flower stems start to lift up their gay balls of bloom. If the weather turns bitter, as it is likely to do, the stems huddle near the earth, but when the warm sun comes out they grow and grow. Although they start blooming as soon as they're out of the ground, the stems continue to grow to 8 or 10 inches tall, and more and more stalks of flowers are sent up. The leaves also lengthen, gradually forming an upstanding head of crinkled, toothed, rather downy foliage."

Two pulmonarias also thrive in moist shady sites and make pleasing additions to the early March scene in Zones 3 to 6. The 6- to 12-inch cowslip lungwort, *Pulmonaria angustifolia*, and the 6- to 18-inch Bethlehem sage, *P. saccharata*, offer drooping pink, trumpet-shaped clusters that gradually change to blue. 'Pink Dawn' and the rose-colored 'Mrs. Moon' are varieties of the Bethlehem sage; a white variety is also available, and the leaves are white-spotted. Grow new plants from spring-sown seeds or from fall divisions of old plants. Nice for naturalizing, these European pulmonarias are good companions for chionodoxas that like similar conditions.

Late Winter Wild Flowers

Spring-beauty, *Claytonia virginica*, one of our lovely native plants, usually opens its delicate white-to-pink blooms as early as March and goes on crowning its thin stems with loose flower clusters until June. The acid leaf mold of a lightly shaded wild garden suits this plant with grassy foliage to perfection. It's a good idea to indicate its location with a couple of plant markers, for it disappears totally in summer.

In fairly deep shade you can enjoy a charming duet of round-leaved hepaticas, *Hepatica americana*, and maidenhair ferns, which push their fronds through early. The lilac-white or rose flowers of the hepaticas resemble anemones and offer a pleasant contrast in form to the ferns. Since hepaticas self-sow freely, it is easy to have a pretty colony quite quickly in a shaded corner of your woodland. Unlike most wild flowers, hepaticas favor a dry location, with acid soil, of course.

A handsomely sculptured plant, the skunk cabbage, *Symplocarpus foetidus*, belongs on the banks of a stream or in other damp areas; there its early brownish and pale green emergence in March will notify you that winter is on the wane. Taller than most other early wild plants, this reaches to 2 feet—that is, the foliage does; the hooded flowers are scarcely visible among the broad, unfolding leaf clumps. And incidentally, there is no smell of skunk unless the leaves are cut. This native flourishes in light shade and is well worth your acquaintance.

The March appearance of the solitary white flowers of our native bloodroot, *Sanguinaria canadensis*, thrusting through unfolding, broad, feltlike leaves marks the end of winter. Like many other wild flowers of early appearance, these are gone by May. Plants thrive in rich soil in light to quite deep shade and do well even under broad-leaved shrubs like laurel; bloodroot self-sows freely.

The native round-leaved yellow violet, *Viola rotundifolia*, is a treasure for moist, cool, lightly shaded woodsy areas. The early yellow, purple-striped flowers may surprise you as they open on the heels of the snow. Plants thrive under shrubs and evergreens as well as in woodlands and their enduring foliage makes a pleasing ground cover there.

Viola tricolor hortensis, the European wild pansy or Johnny-jump-up, a parent of our garden pansies, is an annual or short-lived perennial growing 2 inches high and offering all the luscious pansy hues in smaller flowers. It is easy from seed and sometimes blooms in midwinter. My favorite true violet, *Viola cornuta*, and the

The snow trillium (*T. grandiflorum*) in some beneficent winters opens late-March blooms in a setting of ivy and myrtle. *Taloumis photo*

apricot variety, 'Chantreyland', may bloom in late winter, and if cut sternly back and fertilized, they may open new blossoms in the fall and then safely winter over. Have an eye to your pansy plants whenever they are set out and you are very likely to be surprised by some midwinter blooms.

One of the handsomest of wild flowers is the snow trillium, *Trillium grandiflorum*; in mild winters it may bloom *late* in March. Depending on your passion for winter flowers, it is worth planting for its white-to-rose flowers; place it in a woodland setting, a rock garden, or the semishade of a protecting evergreen shrub.

Christmas Roses and Other Winter Flowers

NAME	ZONE	HEIGHT IN INCHES	COLOR AND SEASON	CULTURE	REMARKS
Adonis amurensis Amur Adonis or Pheasant's-Eye	3–7	18	Yellow flowers, almost 2″ across; sometimes emerges through snow.	Woods soil, with full sun or light shade. Sow seeds in fall.	Both are most welcome earlies; nice with snowdrops.
A. vernalis Spring Adonis	3–8	12–18	Yellow flowers, almost 3″ across; blooms Mar.–Apr. Ferny foliage.		Has been used medicinally. 'Alba' has white flowers.
Bergenia ciliata (*ligulata*) Winter Begonia	3–8	12	Nodding white, pink, or purple flowers; blooms late Mar. Rounded, sometimes evergreen leaves.	Moist, partial shade; cover lightly in winter in very cold areas.	Nice with trout lilies and evergreen ferns.
Bethlehem Sage, see *Pulmonaria* Bloodroot, see *Sanguinaria* Christmas Rose, see *Helleborus*					
Claytonia virginica Spring-Beauty	6–8	4–6	Delicate white-to-pink flowers; Mar.–June. Grassy foliage.	Half-shade; acid leaf mold.	Mark the plantings; this disappears in summer but is a good spring ground cover. Native.
Cowslip Lungwort, see *Pulmonaria*					

Helleborus—species listed below			Blooms Dec.–May.	Open humusy soil; winter sun, open summer shade, or continuous light shade under deep-rooted trees. Resents disturbance.	Handsome, almost evergreen plants. Time of bloom depends on zone, age, and a protected location. Water in dry spells; light fertilizing late Sept.
H. foetidus Setterwort	6–8	24	Purple-tipped green flowers; mid-Jan.		Tall stems rise from 12-inch mounds of ferny, evergreen foliage; shrublike.
H. lividus corsicus Corsican Hellebore	7–9	18	Small, cupped green flowers, Feb.–Mar. Nice for St. Patrick's Day arrangements.		Architectural foliage is shining and toothed; striking in winter garden; very hardy. (May be listed as H. corsicus.)
H. X sternii	7–9	18			Leaves have fewer teeth, slight marbling; rare in this country.
H. niger Christmas Rose	3–7	12	Here Jan.–May; flowers pure white to deep pink; blooms before and after snow.		Indispensable winter perennial.
H. n. 'Altifolius'		12–15			A tall, larger-flowering variety of H. niger; blooms to 5" across.

NAME	ZONE	HEIGHT IN INCHES	COLOR AND SEASON	CULTURE	REMARKS
Hepatica americana Round-lobed Hepatica	4–7	6	Anemonelike, lilac, white, or rose-colored flowers; mid-Mar.–Apr.; evergreen foliage.	Dry, acid soil; light or quite deep shade.	Self-sows freely; makes pretty colonies in shady corners or inter-planted with ferns. Native.
Pansy, see *Viola*					
Pheasant's-Eye, see *Adonis*					
Primrose, see *Primula*					
Primula denticulata Himalayan Primrose	4–5	8–10	Lavender, pink, or purple flowers in dense globes, on stout stems; usually blooms right after snow melts, before foliage develops.	Best where winters are cold; semishaded slope ideal; good drainage essential.	Reliable and enchanting. A white form, 'Alba', has slightly larger flowers in looser heads.
Pulmonaria angustifolia Cowslip Lungwort	3–6	6–12	Small blue trumpet flowers; Mar.	Good for naturalizing in shade; moist, humusy soil; easy from spring-sown seeds.	Grow new plants from spring-sown seeds or divide old plants in fall.
P. saccharata Bethlehem Sage		6–18	Drooping pink clusters in Mar. changing to blue; leaves mottled with white.		'Pink Dawn', rose 'Mrs. Moon', and white varieties all attractive, pretty with chionodoxas.

Name			Flowers	Conditions	Notes
Sanguinaria canadensis Bloodroot	3–6	3–6	Single, white 1½″ flowers; Mar.–May; broad, feltlike leaves.	Light to deep shade; rich soil.	Disappears in summer; valued for its very early, evanescent flowers. Native.
Skunk Cabbage, see *Symplocarpus* Spring Beauty, see *Claytonia*					
Symplocarpus foetidus Skunk Cabbage	3–7	12–24	Inconspicuous hooded flowers; Mar. Handsome, big leaf clumps.	Light shade; moist or wet soil, as along a brook; very effective.	No smell unless cut. Green plants open slowly but very early; cut these back as they fade. Disappears in summer. Native.
Viola rotundifolia Round-leaved Yellow Violet	3–5	4–6	Early pale yellow flowers follow the snow.	For moist, cool woods; half to deep shade; not for hot sun.	Thrives under shrubs and evergreens; a great joy. Native.
V. tricolor hortensis Johnny-Jump-Up or European Wild Pansy	4–6	8–12	Purple shades, yellow, white, garnet; really an annual or short-lived perennial.	Likes it cool; sometimes blooms in winter, always blooms in early spring and fall if cut back after first spring bloom and fertilized.	Easy from seed. Often winters over, especially from a spring sowing.
Violet, see *Viola* Winter Begonia, see *Bergenia*					

Early fall is an excellent time to plant spring-flowering bulbs. Catalogues like this usually include pictures in color that can help you plan attractive garden effects. *Fitch photo*

3

The Intrepid Minor Bulbs

THE TINY BULBS THAT BLOOM from late January through March are a rare delight and are "minor" only in that their flowers are for the most part quite small. The pleasure they provide is considerable, for they offer the brightest possible flowers —yellow, lavender, purple, white, and a few pinks—at a time when there is little color competition in the yard and garden. Inexpensive, they multiply rapidly, so that a dozen or so become a noticeable drift, especially among the stones and winter foliages of a rock garden. To get the earliest possible blooms, try to provide a "warm" soil. As Louise Beebe Wilder has pointed out, "A clay soil, remember, is cold and discourages early awakening, whereas a warm soil is as good as an alarm clock." If yours is extremely clayey you can, of course, improve it with sand and compost and so promote earlier bloom.

Aconites

Whether the winter aconites, *Eranthis hyemalis*, will open their green-ruffed golden cups in January or not until February depends on location as well as the severity of the winter. Our winters vary so much from quite mild to extremely cold. First bloom for me has come in late January or early February, in beds to

33

the south of the house and close to a cellar window-well, also in sheltered nooks on a terrace fully open to the eastern sun.

Because the heavy hand of winter still hangs over the garden, these bright, free-flowering aconites always cause a lot of excitement. Visitors are fascinated and exclaim, especially if the aconites are associated with Christmas roses that are also in full bloom. Because aconites bloom so early, it's wise to set out the small tubers just as soon as you get them—late August or early September—so order early. Upon receiving them, soak the tubers overnight if they appear the least bit shriveled, then plant them. Once they are established, count on their seeding themselves freely and spreading most acceptably.

Irises

Iris danfordiae, a reticulata form and one of the bulbous irises, might also open January flowers. More dependably, this and other miniature irises bloom in the sun on February and March days and there certainly afford you winter excitement. Less familiar than other early bulbs, these treasures from the Caucasus have not been easily come by in the past, but some are now offered by growers—though not by any means all the winter irises we might enjoy.

Although I rarely favor mixtures, I suggest that if you don't know these little early gems, you might experiment with a collection of *I. reticulata* and its forms. The lightly scented, violet-blue, gold-touched flowers of the species grow to about 5 inches, with the leaves eventually stretching to 18 inches. 'Clairette' is a lighter blue shade; the hybrid 'Joyce' is blue with an orange central ridge; the pale blue 'Springtime' has dark blue falls and small white blotches. A reticulata mixture is likely to include plants with flowers from pale blue to reddish purple, a small pleasing panorama for your rock garden or at the foot of an early shrub like the winter honeysuckle. To brighten the effect, do add *I. danfordiae*, the bright canary-yellow reticulata from Asia Minor.

Plant all these bulbous irises as early in fall as you can get them, but set danfordiae 6 inches deep instead of the usual 3 inches, with the hope that the bulbs will not split after blooming as they do at the usual 3 inches. If they do split, it's best to replace them every year, for it's too much bother and too uncertain as to time of bloom to try to give them special handling. The darker colors need a light setting, such as the gray-toned snow-in-summer, *Cerastium tomen-*

tosum, perhaps, rather than a setting of evergreens. These little irises do not *require* full sun, but they are likely to bloom earlier in a sheltered, sunny place, one that is, of course, well drained. The winter aconites, winter crocuses, and snowdrops can be their delightful companions in rock-garden pockets or in drifts of one color along your shrub border.

Molly Price, an iris specialist, advises protection in colder regions. From her own garden in Rockland County, New York (Zone 5), she reports: "I cover them lightly, as soon as the ground is well frozen, with evergreen boughs over the oak leaves that blow onto my garden. A mulch of salt hay would serve the same purpose, which is to inhibit too early emergence. Left to themselves, they might bloom in January and be unable to survive the remaining long weeks of winter."

Two other bulbous irises would give you pleasure if only you could locate a supply. *I. histrio* is usually earlier than *I. reticulata*. The short-stemmed bright violet flowers, with a central white mark or white-blotched area and falls with a yellow ridge, open on short stems, but the leaves grow to 12 inches. Also early is *I. histrioides* with china-blue flowers. The variety 'Major' is particularly recommended; it is a strong blue, with gold-and-white markings on almost horizontal falls.

Snowdrops, Snowflakes, and Scillas

Snowdrops, *Galanthus*, undaunted by snow, are also winter jewels opening their pure white pendent cups right after the aconites, sometimes along with them. Try to get your order filled by August or early September, so that the little bulbs can have a long growing period. Surely snowdrops are among the most permanent of bulbs, and they bloom a long time. From my bedroom windows I enjoy a great patch that covers a high sunny ledge. I feel sure that they are what is left of a garden planted there perhaps a half century ago. These are the old-fashioned single *G. nivalis*. The less graceful double form—'Flore Pleno'—and the larger-flowering *G. elwesii* are both worth growing, especially in great patches of woodland under deciduous trees. Snowdrops are sturdy flowers, lasting a long while in bloom, so that you can plan a tapestry with these and aconites along with the bright blue 4-inch *Hyacinthus ciliatus* (*Bellevalia ciliata*) that opens early in March. A pleasant associate would also be *Chionodoxa*, so aptly named the glory-of-the-snow. *C. luciliae* emerges through snow, even ice, and the white-centered lavender stars are well set off by a ground cover of low phlox or candytuft.

It is a good plan to increase your stock of snowdrops right after they bloom. Replanting them then pays off in a much bigger crop. Of course, it would be fine if you could get snowdrops to plant in March from a bulb specialist, but that is rather doubtful, his stock usually lasting only until late fall.

A friend who is particularly taken with these snowdrops imports some of the less usual kinds from the Dutch firm of Van Tubergen Ltd. (Haarlem, Holland). V. Sackville-West wrote enthusiastically of these:

"It is as well to remember that they are different kinds besides the common snowdrop (only one hates to call it common). For instance, there is the finer variety called *Galanthus nivalis viridi-apice*, or green-tipped. Then there is the tall, large-flowered *Galanthus elwesii*, from the hills behind Smyrna, often seen in old cottage gardens but not so often planted by the modern gardener, a most graceful dangling thing, flowering rather later than the little *Galanthus nivalis*, the 'milk-flower of the snow.' For people who want something really unusual, and are prepared to pay for it, there is *G. ikariae*, which has the romantic peculiarity of growing in a wild state in only one place in the world: the small island of Ikaria or Nikaria in the Aegean Sea, where Hercules buried the ill-fated Icarus. It flowers in March, and much resembles the common snowdrop, except that the flower is a little larger and the leaves curl over backwards."

The less spectacular, but charming, spring meadow saffron, *Bulbocodium vernum*, with its pink-lavender crocuslike blooms, opens about the same time—that is, February into March—and might be planted near the snowdrops and snowflakes. The enchanting spring snowflake, *Leucojum vernum*, is another fine choice. Of touching delicacy, each single, bell-shaped, dangling flower is a green-tipped white. Plant enough of these for picking; indoors, their vaguely violet scent is even more noticeable than it is outdoors.

Of the squills, or scilla bulbs, two with blue flowers can now bring darker hues to the early panorama. The deep blue *Scilla bifolia* opens earliest; paler blue with a silvery background, *S. tubergeniana* opens a little later. *S. sibirica* and its varieties—the large, bright blue 'Spring Beauty' and the white 'Alba'—do not bloom until well into March. If given adequate watering, squills will self-sow and increase surprisingly. I enjoy them in a ring planting under a dogwood tree. The 6-inch-high scillas are reliable bulbs, naturalizing nicely where a ground cover is wanted, or growing in colonies in the rock garden.

These yellow species crocuses in a naturalized setting bloom well ahead of the larger Dutch varieties. *Taloumis photo*

The Colorful Winter Crocuses

Essential in the winter garden are the crocuses, especially those species that, given a sunny place and some protection, prove so dependable for early blooming, from February into March. These species include the glowing yellow *Crocus susianus* (*angustifolius*), called 'Cloth-of-Gold'; the lilac-to-purple *C. sieberi*, especially 'Firefly'; and that great favorite, the silvery lavender Tommy crocus, *C. tomasinianus*. I always get winter amusement from the 7-foot strip of these that I have planted inside an edging of hardy candytuft, with the further protection of a cellar window-well and the house wall. It is a clear example of what sunlight will do, for although the whole row faces south, half the strip blooms ten days before the other half, because of the way the sun strikes.

Among the many faithful crocuses, you are bound to find your own favorites, and you will discover all sorts of small areas for them—but not in the lawn, I hope. There they must either be cut down to accommodate the mower *before* their foliage is ripe, or be left to ripen while the lawn looks shabbier and shabbier awaiting its first cut. Swaths of yellow crocuses will be effective in front of your shrubbery borders—not at the very rim, but just inside some low edging plants. Or you may want to use them as I have—placing *C. susianus* groups of about a dozen or so in between Christmas ferns.

In your garden the lovely lilac-colored *C. imperati*, with its musty-honey scent, may be the first to open; or the prolific, long-lasting, orange-yellow Ankara crocus, *C. ancyrensis*, may bloom first. You may find your favorite crocus among the *C. chrysanthus* hybrids of blue, cream, or yellow; or the star-shaped orange-yellow *C. korolkowii* from Turkestan; or the so-called Cloth-of-Silver crocus, *C. versicolor* 'picturatus', of the Maritime Alps, lilac or pure white with rich purple feathering.

C. vernus is the common or Dutch crocus, lavender or white with purple stripes. Among the varieties you probably know is the silver-striped lilac 'Pickwick'. The familiar and very reliable Dutch crocuses produce larger, usually later blooms than the other species, though in some propitious years they, too, open soon enough in March to be included in our winter calendar.

Other Colorful Winter Possibilities

Opening soon after the first crocus, the Grecian windflower or Greek anemone —*Anemone blanda*, the delight of early spring visitors to Greece—is covered with 2-inch daisylike blooms of blue, pink, or white. The selection 'Atrocaerulea' produces deep blue flowers with prominent yellow stamens. 'Radar' contributes bright red flowers; 'White Splendour' has handsome larger blooms. The ferny foliage offers a pretty setting for the flowers.

The gray tubers require the same early planting as winter aconites (to which they are related), and the same presoaking if tubers appear dry or shriveled. For earliest bloom, pick a sheltered spot, especially as these windflowers unexpectedly do not appear at their best in a windy site. The blossoms fold up on sunless days or when the temperature falls. As the March weather improves, the flowers expand their rays and offer bright color for more than a month. These winter anemones will be a dramatic addition to your cold-weather garden and look lovely under your gray-budded dogwood tree.

An early March, sometimes February, blue is *Hyacinthus ciliatus*. This used to be called *Muscari azureum*, and it does resemble the grape hyacinth. It has a fringed leaf and associates pleasantly with the other early bulbs.

The *Narcissus* plants are variable in their blooming times, but three species are likely to bring color to the winter scene. My tiny yellow trumpet one, formerly *N. minimus* and now called *N. asturiensis,* may bloom early with the snowdrops. Planted on a sunny bank, the 'February Gold' variety of the frilled *N. cyclameneus* has often lived up to its name for me. And although the charming hoop-petticoat daffodil, *N. bulbocodium,* so familiar to us at Colonial Williamsburg, sometimes doesn't bloom until the end of March, for all of us bent on having color in our winter gardens, it is worth trying, if only for transition into early spring.

The striped squill, *Puschkinia scilloides,* with its pendent blue-striped milk-white bells and a gentle mignonette fragrance, is among the bulbs I have grown most delightfully with my tiny, very early daffodil, *N. asturiensis*. These two, so delicate in form, presented a miniature scene beside a flagstone walk and always seemed to me to require a tiny statue to complete the effect.

A delightful but very chancy choice is the coum cyclamen; like the hellebores, it is not for the impatient. A smaller edition of the florists' cyclamen, this takes time to establish and may not show up the first winter even after a July planting. My own does not add up to a paean of praise but yours may be better. Once established, a patch of the coum cyclamen opening in February or March is a winter-garden spectacular. The type is a brilliant rose red, but there is also a white form.

The trout lily, *Erythronium americanum,* may open its minute lily-formed yellow flowers before March 21 closes our book. It is best naturalized in a damp

For February and March color. ABOVE LEFT: Purple-striped white 'Pickwick' crocus. ABOVE RIGHT: Tiny gray-blue *Puschkinia*. BELOW LEFT: Water lily tulip, *Tulipa kaufmanniana*. RIGHT: Snowdrops, *Galanthus. Malak photos*

The yellow petticoat narcissus (*N. bulbocodium*) offers flowers of charmingly different form from the more familiar narcissus, but it may not open till the end of March. *Malak photo*

area, though you must remember to look for it, for the blooms are not conspicuous there, rising only a few inches above the mottled brown-and-green leaves. It is a small something that volunteered near my brook and gave me much pleasure through the years. Another species, *E. californicum*, grows to a foot, the flowers larger, creamy white, and variously marked with mahogany; and it does surprisingly well in the eastern states.

Tulips belong more to spring than winter, but if they tend to be *your* flower there are three species that are naturally quite early. The one called Violet Queen, *Tulipa pulchella*, usually blooms by the end of February and is a pretty violet-pink with a yellow base. Then there is the red-marked white water lily tulip, *T. kaufmanniana*, and the green-to-brown-flushed *T. biflora turkestanica* with the distinction of four to five flowers to each stem. These two are for March.

Bulbs for very likely winter bloom may not have occurred to you before, but they will give you a great deal of pleasure through the cold months once you

The trout lily, *Erythronium americanum*, naturalized in a damp area, has often bloomed for me before the end of winter. *Malak photo*

get acquainted with their colorful possibilities. Tuck in colonies of them, great or small, in your garden—along your foundation planting, or as edging for the big shrubs in your yard. In this chapter I have included the dependables and the maybes. If you have not previously been tempted by these delightful early birds, plant five or six kinds in your warmest, out-of-the-wind spots, and I am sure winter will bring you some unexpected garden color.

The winter aconites, *Eranthis hyemalis*—often blooming as early as late January—are golden treasures for the cold-weather garden. *Malak photo*

Bulbs for Winter Flowers

NAME	ZONE	HEIGHT IN INCHES	TIME OF BLOOM	DESCRIPTION	COMMENT
Aconites, see *Eranthis*					
Anemone blanda Greek Windflower	6–8	3–6	Feb.–Mar.	Mixture includes blue, pink, white daisylike flowers; ferny foliage; tuberous rooted.	Plant tubers 2″ to 3″ deep, 4″ apart; withstands bad weather; needs summer shade, humusy soil, winter sun. 'White Splendour', red 'Radar', dark blue 'Atrocaerulea' are fine selections.
Bulbocodium vernum Spring Meadow Saffron	4–8	6	Feb.–Mar.	Pink-lavender, crocuslike, stemless flowers; interesting, not the greatest.	Plant 3″ deep, 2″ to 3″ apart; likes sun to light shade. Foliage up to 6″ appears after flowers.
Chionodoxa luciliae Glory-of-the-Snow	4–8	6	Early Mar. but sometimes with aconites.	Lavender color, 5 or more white-centered flowers on each stem. Also, white 'Alba' variety.	Plant 3″ deep, 2″ apart; endures Mar. snow. Good for naturalizing in relatively sunny places.

Crocus—vernal-flowering species listed below	3–6	All bloom early Feb.–Mar. if given spring sunshine and protective warmth of a wall.	All have grassy foliage.	Plant early, 2″ to 3″ deep, 5″ to 6″ apart.
C. *ancyrensis* Ankara Crocus	5–8		Deep orange.	Usually earliest, in late winter.
C. *chrysanthus* hybrids	5–8		Cream, golden-yellow.	Very free-flowering, some striped brown.
C. *imperati*	4–8		Lilac or white, purple feathered.	May be the first to open.
C. *korolkowii* Celandine Crocus	6–8		Orange-yellow.	From Turkestan and Afghanistan; star-shaped. Good rock-garden plant.
C. *sieberi*	6–8		Lilac to purple shades.	'Firefly' variety is lilac-pink.
C. *susianus* (*angustifolius*)	4–7		Glowing yellow; starlike flowers.	Called Cloth-of-Gold; early blooms and in succession from each corm.
C. *tomasinianus*	5–8		Pale lavender, silvery-gray outside.	Tommy crocus; fine hybrids. Elegant form.

NAME	ZONE	HEIGHT IN INCHES	TIME OF BLOOM	DESCRIPTION	COMMENT
C. vernus Common or Dutch Crocus	4–8			Lilac or white with purple stripes.	Common crocus, always satisfactory, with petals generally larger than in other species.
C. v. 'Golden Yellow'				Fine color.	Very old variety.
C. v. 'Paulus Potter'				Excellent purple.	Free-flowering.
C. v. 'Pickwick'				Lilac, striped silver.	My favorite; blooms profusely, long-lasting.
C. versicolor 'Picturatus'	5–8			Lilac or white with purple markings.	Called Cloth-of-Silver.
Cyclamen orbiculatum	5–9	3–4	Dec.–Mar.	Rose, red, or white; small editions of the florist type.	Plant corms 1½" deep, preferably in July, in light shade; mark the spots—plants often disappear for a time. Give protection where winters are severe.

C. coum Coum Cyclamen	6–9	2–3	Feb.–Mar.	Leaves appear in fall and stay green all winter.	From the Turkish island of Cous. White 'Album' variety especially fine.
Daffodil, see *Narcissus* Dutch Crocus, see *Crocus vernus*					
Eranthis hyemalis Winter Aconite	4–6	8	Late Jan.–Feb.	Golden yellow, with green ruff. Buttercup family.	Plant tubers in early Sept., 2″ deep, 2″ apart; rich soil. Soak overnight first if shriveled; indispensable for winter bloom.
Erythronium americanum Trout Lily	3–9	6–8	Mar.–June.	Tiny yellow, pink, lavender, or white nodding, lilylike flowers; mottled brown-and-green leaves. Good in mixture.	Plant tubers 2″ to 3″ deep, 4″ apart; best naturalized in rich soil in a damp place with light shade. Western species among the best. Do not pick the leaf; each plant has only two, depends on those for its life.

NAME	ZONE	HEIGHT IN INCHES	TIME OF BLOOM	DESCRIPTION	COMMENT
Galanthus elwesii Giant Snowdrop	4–9	6–9	Late Jan.–Feb., right after aconites.	Large white, single flowers.	Plant all snowdrops in Sept., 4″ deep, 2″ apart. Plants recover even after snow. Attractive in broad woodland plantings; require early sunshine.
G. e. 'Flore Pleno'		4–6		Double flowers.	
G. nivalis Common Snowdrop	4–9	4–6		Single flowers.	
Glory-of-the-Snow, see *Chionodoxa* Hoop-Petticoat Daffodil, see *Narcissus*					
Hyacinthus ciliatus (*Bellevalia ciliata*)	5–7	18	Early Mar.	Resembles grape hyacinth with cone-shaped cluster of brilliant blue, open bells; narrow leaves fringed along the margins.	Plant 3″ deep, 4″ to 5″ apart; sometimes appears early Feb. Will grow in places later densely shaded by trees.
Iris—bulbous species listed below	5–7			Leaves to 18″, die down in May, endure snow.	Grow these with snowdrops, winter crocuses, and winter aconites; plant 3″ to 4″ deep (but 6″ for *bakerana*), 3″ to 4″ apart.

Above: Winter Forms and Traceries (Franklin photo).

Left: European Cranberry Bush (Hampfler photo).

Above: Small-leaved Cotoneaster (Taloumis photo).

Below: Christmas Rose (Fitch photo).

Left: Corsican Hellebore (Fitch photo).

Below left: Pheasant's-Eye Adonis (Hampfler photo).

Below right: Himalayan Primrose (Franklin photo).

Above: Glory-of-the-Snow.   *Below left:* Netted Iris.
Below right: Narcissus Cyclameneus (all Hampfler photos).

Left: Snowdrops and Winter Aconites.

Below: Grecian Windflower (both Hampfler photos).

Opposite page, above: Spring Snowflake.

Opposite page, below left: Golden Weeping Willow (Swinehart photo).

Opposite page, below right: Washington Thorn (Taloumis photo).

Top: Japanese Black Pine.

Above: Blue Jay at Breakfast (both Fitch photos).

Left: Siberian Dogwood Shrub (Franklin photo).

Below left: American Holly (Fitch photo).

Below right: Chinese Witch Hazel (Taloumis photo).

I. bakerana	5–9	4	Feb.	Purple, white.	Light violet scent.
I. danfordiae	5–8	2–3	Jan.–Mar.	Yellow flowers, green at base.	Sometimes late Jan.
I. reticulata Netted Iris	5–8	4–7	Jan.	Deep violet with yellow blotch.	Lightly scented, charming in rock gardens. 'Clairette', 'Joyce', 'Springtime' are lovely hybrids in pale and deep shades. *I. histrio* and *I. histrioides*, Feb.–Mar.— desirable but difficult to obtain.
Leucojum vernum Spring Snowflake	4–8	6–9	Feb.–Mar.	Green-tipped white flowers, bell-shaped and single.	Plant 3″ deep, 3″ to 4″ apart; delicate and charming.
Meadow Saffron, see *Bulbocodium*					
Narcissus asturiensis (*minimus*) Daffodil	4–9	3–5	Mar.	Tiny yellow trumpet-type flower.	A treasure for those who delight in miniature forms; blooms with snowdrops and *Puschkinia*.

NAME	ZONE	HEIGHT IN INCHES	TIME OF BLOOM	DESCRIPTION	COMMENT
N. bulbocodium Hoop-Petticoat Daffodil	6–9	15	Late Mar.	Golden hoop-petticoat type; rushlike foliage.	This one doesn't always make winter; variety 'Conspicuus' is larger flowered form.
N. cyclameneus	6–9	8	Feb.–Mar.	Rich yellow, frilled, trumpet-type flowers.	Fine for naturalizing. 'February Gold' to 12" noteworthy; these need a damp soil.
Puschkinia scilloides Striped Squill	3–7	4–6	Late Mar.	Pendent blue-striped, milk-white bells. 'Alba' all white.	Plant 2" to 3" deep, 4" to 5" apart; should be more frequently planted; delightful and early. Best in cold climates.
Scilla—species listed below Squill	4–9	6			Plant 2" deep, 3" to 4" apart; naturalizes; good with a ground cover.
S. bifolia	4–9	6	Feb.	Deep blue. Also, varieties 'Alba' and 'Rosea'.	Earliest, usually with winter aconites.
S. sibirica	4–8	6	Mar.	Bright blue.	'Alba', white; 'Spring Beauty', larger electric-blue flowers.

S. tubergeniana	4–8	5	Feb.–Mar.	Delicate blue on silvery background.	Nice for clumps in rockery. This and *sibirica* not for hot climates.
Snowdrop, see *Galanthus* Snowflake, see *Leucojum* Squill, see *Scilla* Striped Squill, see *Puschkinia* Trout Lily, see *Erythronium*					
Tulipa—species listed below Tulip					Plant 3″ to 4″ deep, 4″ to 6″ apart.
T. biflora	4–7	8–10	Mar.	Two white-and-yellow flowers per stem, each ¾″ across.	Var. *turkestanica* 4 to 8 somewhat larger flowers. Enjoys a lime soil.
T. kaufmanniana Water Lily Tulip	3–7	5–10	Late Mar.	Creamy white with red or yellow markings.	Really delightful. Plant 6″ deep.
T. pulchella 'Violacea'	4–7	4–8	Mid-Mar.	Violet-pink with a yellow or sometimes black base.	Sometimes called Violet Queen.
Windflower, Greek, see *Anemone*					

The Cornelian cherry, *Cornus mas*, dots every leafless branch with yellow fluffs of bloom in March. *Taloumis photo*

4

Small Trees and Shrubs
for Winter Color

WOODY PLANTS THAT BLOOM in winter are an unbelievable delight. To my knowl-
edge there aren't more than eight fairly reliable ones, but until you have tried
others, you won't know whether some of the doubtfuls will also perform well
for you under favorable conditions of sun and shelter—*and in a benign winter.*
Some seasons are more propitious than others, but the adventurous gardener
considers the game worth the candle when February and March offer flowers—
and fine fragrance too—despite a touch of snow.

My own experience here in Zone 6 has been most rewarding. Temperatures
rarely reach the allowed minus 10 degrees for this area, so that—with these
trees, shrubs, and a vine—I can truly claim I have flowers from January on.
Again, to gauge the winter possibilities of these plants for your place, locate your
zone on the endpaper map.

The heath *Erica carnea* 'Springwood White', a low-spreading evergreen, is one of the first shrubs to bloom in winter. Sempervivums fill in the rock crevices. *Taloumis photo*

Winter Dependables

The heaths are the first and bravest; I do enjoy the low-spreading evergreen cultivars of *Erica carnea*, hardy in Zone 6. Strategically planted near the house wall and in front of the pink-and-white Christmas roses, the 'Springwood Pink' heather provides an arresting winter drama. 'Springwood White' and the gray-leaved 'Silver Queen' thrive on a little slope protected from the wind by tall laurel bushes. None of these exceeds 8 inches. 'King George' grows to 12 inches and is most reliable, but its strident magenta puts me off. You might like 'Vivelii' with flowers and foliage both purple; this blooms in March. The taller, lavender-pink *E. X darleyensis* is the longest-blooming heath species, from November throughout the winter—a nice record indeed.

Wintersweet, *Chimonanthus praecox*, supposedly winter-hardy only in the South, as in Zone 9, offers its fragrant bloom much farther north, certainly as far as Philadelphia (Zone 6), where ancient specimens survive. The stemless flowers perched on gray twigs open sheer yellow late in February. Afternoon sun and protection from wind in January and February are essential. Hardly a handsome specimen, wintersweet is best planted in an inconspicuous corner where it will usually supply not only fragrant winter flowers outdoors but always perfumed cuttings for indoor bouquets.

The Cornelian cherry, *Cornus mas*, has delighted me for years with its yellow fluffs of bloom dotting every leafless branch in March. Since the flower buds on this dogwood species are present all winter, clippings of this one are also easy to force indoors. A spreading plant, the Cornelian cherry can reach a wide 15 feet even in Zone 4, but I like it pruned narrow and upright to make a small tree, so that I can crowd other early performers into the same bed, which is opposite the kitchen window. An excellent border or accent shrub, the Cornelian cherry produces plum-shaped, red summer fruits that make excellent jelly.

Other dogwoods, hardy in the north to Zone 2, are outstanding in the winter garden because of their colorful bark. The Siberian *Cornus alba* 'Sibirica' is bright coral-red; the red-osier dogwood, *C. sericea*, is a darker shade; and one of its varieties, 'Flaviramea', produces a vivid yellow display. Silhouetted against the snow, these shrubs are an arresting sight. Prune vigorously in spring to promote growth of young shoots, as these are the most colorful.

The witch hazels, *Hamamelis*, are certain to be winter delights in Zone 6, and again yellow is their color. A planting of the native *H. vernalis* grew near a seat at the edge of my former Round Garden and reached 6 feet there. In propitious years it was a golden, late-February surprise. In my friend's Philadelphia garden, in a northern situation, buds open on the first mild day of January and the short yellow or orange curls continue to unfurl for about two months.

The Chinese witch hazel, *H. mollis*, a taller species with larger flowers, is situated beside a stone wall in my garden, where it waits for a warm spell late in February or early March to unroll its marvelous ribbons of bloom with its pure delicious fragrance of jonquils. If the weather turns icy cold, it rolls them right up again. It fails to bloom only in rare years of unusual cold when the buds do not survive the January freeze. It is well worth planting, as most seasons are successful, especially when it blooms at the same time as the wintersweet shrubs

The winter honeysuckle shrub, *Lonicera fragrantissima*, attractive year round, is covered from late February to April with tiny white blooms of marvelous sweetness. *Taloumis photo*

with their exquisite honeysuckle scent. In fall the leaves turn a glowing yellow.

Winter jasmine, *Jasminum nudiflorum*, for Zone 5, is a rambling subshrub that grows to 15 feet in height but is best treated as a vine. Mine is fastened, espalier-fashion, to the south wall of the house, where the yellow blooms open continuously on bright green whiplike stems for some weeks from mid-March on. If cold kills the first flowers, more open in the sun, and I enjoy the contrast this thin, flowering winter vine from China makes with the broader shrubs. Prunings make nice yellow bouquets for the house all through winter.

Crab apples with a light covering of snow are effective accents on each side of a driveway. *Krieg photo*

Long dear to my heart is the winter honeysuckle, *Lonicera fragrantissima*, wonderfully scented and suggesting some roses. In my old garden I grew it at a corner of the house and let it grow tall. Here in my small formal garden it rambles narrowly along a fence, sheltering a Christmas rose below. The scent of the profuse tiny blooms carries for yards from late February to April. Bloom usually occurs before the leaves open, though sometimes this shrub proves evergreen. It can grow to 15 feet and is particularly attractive pruned to an open fountain form. In sun or semishade, even in a northern location in Zone 6, this fragrant honeysuckle has performed reliably year in and year out. It is perhaps my favorite winter-flowering shrub.

Late in March, the French pussy willow, *Salix caprea*, produces silver-pink catkins that are deliciously honey-scented. Soon these are covered by lemon-yellow stamens, more than 2 inches long, and these give the tree a lovely luminous air. This is the pussy willow sold by florists as cut "flowers" in winter. But from February on, you can force your own cuttings in vases of water, where they readily root. Set out in a hedgerow or as single specimens, these cuttings grow in a few years to 20 feet, if you leave them unpruned and permit them to reach such a height. My tree flourished beside the brook, where it was kept low by drastic yearly cutbacks; the prunings were thrust into the bank. There they

The native pussy willow, *Salix discolor*, is the delight of children when the pearly catkins "bloom" in February. *Genereux photo*

soon became bushes. (However, this tree also thrives in dry as well as swampy soils and even in city gardens.) Our native pussy willow, *S. discolor*, has the advantage of earlier February "bloom" and is hardy to parts of Zone 3, but *S. caprea* produces larger, more colorful catkins even in cold Zone 4. Of course, the native pussy willows are the delight of children, for they are among the first trees to look up in spring, and one of the last to admit that summer is finally over.

Sweet box—*Sarcococca hookerana humilis*, an evergreen shrub from the Himalayas—is an excellent cold-weather ground cover with very dark, shining leaves. Hardy in Zones 5 to 7 and only about 18 inches high, this has much to offer the winter garden. The small white flowers with musk-grape fragrance usually open after deep snow and by March in any case.

Other Cold-Weather Possibilities

Those of us who try out some of the small trees and shrubs not really recommended for winter flowering often have delightful surprises, though not every year. A pair of star magnolias, *Magnolia stellata*, trained as broad shrubs, flanked the brick entrance walk in my Philadelphia garden and never failed to bloom there by mid-March. Here in Connecticut in Zone 6, I planted a magnolia in the same bed with the Cornelian cherry tree, protected on the north and open to the south, and the ribbon-petaled, scented, 4-inch flowers rarely opened before late March. The blossoms were perfect for two years out of three and lasted for two to three March-into-April weeks. In unlucky years the flowers turned brown in wet weather; and after one extremely cold winter, my twelve-year-old plant succumbed. However, I did not hesitate to replace it for the lovely chance of the good years.

Perhaps you will be truly adventurous and plant the Japanese apricot, *Prunus mume*, of delicious far-reaching fragrance. Plant-hardy in Zone 6, the snowy blooms opening optimistically in early March warmth often succumb to later cold. Where peaches are hardy, mume, more tree than shrub, usually is also, but I heard one sad tale of a plant—reliable for years and full of fruit—that simply folded and died in a very cold spell in *mid-May*! I remember the day well, for I had to get my heavy winter coat out of camphor when I went to New York.

One evergreen shrub of sweet fragrance is well worth planting for its year-round good looks and the chance of winter flowers. The Chinese leatherleaf mahonia, *Mahonia bealei*, grows to 12 feet in the South and to 3 feet in the North, is plant-hardy in Zone 6, and comes into winter with well-budded flower stems among prickly compound leaves. It is a relative of the barberries. In late February or early March, 6-inch strings of deliciously scented yellow buds open. Partial shade suits this shrub, so popular in Southern gardens, and it requires adequate pruning to keep it shapely.

Less reliably evergreen, the lilac-scented guelder, *Viburnum farreri*, is a member of the marvelous, diversified viburnum clan and is the earliest viburnum to bloom, appearing in late March, before the first forsythias. Buds form the previous autumn, and cut branches will open indoors to make charming bouquets. Outdoors, flowering is brief. This upright shrub is best planted in a protected place. Reports of hardiness vary, but one year I saw thriving plants in bloom in a snowstorm in late March in Toronto, Canada. Anyway, the fragrant guelder is well worth a try in Zone 6 to southern Zone 9 and is reliable farther south.

What to say about the delectable daphnes? When they thrive we cannot praise them too highly, but too often they are a disappointment, disappearing the second or third year after the original, apparently successful, planting. Perhaps we would be happier if we thought of them as "annual evergreens" and considered their brief delight worth their high yearly cost. (The unreliable, but so lovely, 6-inch *Daphne cneorum*, the garland or rose daphne, rarely blooms before mid-May so does not concern us here.)

In mid-March in Philadelphia the fragrant *Magnolia stellata* usually opens its starry blooms; in southern New England in good weather, buds rarely break before late in the month. *Taloumis photo*

The evergreen winter *Daphne odora*, reliably hardy only to Zone 7, is the delight of Southern gardeners. It is considered the most powerfully fragrant of all shrubs, and where it sometimes flourishes in the North, it is greatly prized for its March flowers. This one does not thrive in the acid soil preferred by other evergreens, but no sure cultural regime has yet been developed. A loose soil lightened with sand and limestone is one recipe.

February daphne, *D. mezereum*, despite its name, does not open its heavily creped, richly fragrant, rose-purple or white blooms until late March, but it then offers color and scent through three cold weeks. Native to Europe, it has become naturalized in parts of this country and is the only possibly easy-to-grow daphne. It reaches 3 feet and is hardy in Zone 4; like all daphnes, it is best transplanted when quite small and then grown in high shade.

60

Small Trees and Shrubs for Winter Color

Check your zone on the endpaper map so you can gauge your chances for success with any of these plants.

NAME	ZONE	HEIGHT IN FEET	DESCRIPTION AND FLOWERING TIME	COMMENTS
Chimonanthus praecox Wintersweet	6–9	9	Clear yellow, stemless flowers on gray twigs; Feb.–Mar.	Needs afternoon sun, protection from wind in Jan.–Feb. Likely to perform well if temperatures don't go much below –10°F, as in Zone 6.
Chinese Witch Hazel, see *Hamamelis*				
Cornelian Cherry, see *Cornus*				
Cornus alba 'Sibirica' Siberian Dogwood	2–7	9	Coral-red bark.	These shrubby dogwoods with brilliant winter bark are arresting in silhouette against snow.
C. mas Cornelian Cherry	4–8	20	Small, fluffy yellow flowers; blooms in Mar. before trees are in leaf; red fall fruits.	Branches easy to force indoors since buds are present all winter; good small tree for city conditions.
C. sericea Red-Osier Dogwood	2–7	7	Dark red bark.	Most effective.
C. s. 'Flaviramea'			Vivid yellow bark.	Called golden-twig dogwood.
Darley Heath, see *Erica*				

NAME	ZONE	HEIGHT IN FEET	DESCRIPTION AND FLOWERING TIME	COMMENTS
Erica carnea Spring Heath	5–8	½–1	Small magenta, pink, purple, or white flowers in upright racemes; Jan.–May; needlelike evergreen leaves.	Full sun or partial shade, with acid soil; midsummer buds attractive long before flowers open in winter. Pruning after flowering essential to maintain good form.
E. X darleyensis Darley Heath	6–8	1½	Lilac-pink flowers; Nov. to spring.	Vigorous even under poor conditions.
French Pussy Willow, see *Salix*				
Hamamelis mollis Chinese Witch Hazel	6–8	15	Fragrant yellow flowers (larger than those of *H. vernalis*) have red base; flowers unfurl late Feb.–Mar.; roll up again in very cold spells. Glowing yellow fall leaves.	Neat, rounded shrub; probably best witch hazel if you can have only one.
H. vernalis Spring Witch Hazel	4–8	9	In a well-protected spot red-to-yellow flowers may open Jan. or earlier, otherwise in late Feb.—continuing for 2 months. Usually first winter-flowering shrub.	Small flowers close on a very cold day, then open again for an abundant and fragrant crop. Indispensable native for winter garden in suburban or woodland setting.

Jasminum nudiflorum Winter Jasmine	5–9	15	Yellow flowers on green whiplike stems; if some flowers killed, more open for some weeks late in Mar.	Vine, nice to train against a house wall or fence; prefers a dry, sunny spot.
Lonicera fragrantissima Winter Honeysuckle	6–9	15	Choice winter shrub; abundance of tiny white flowers with marvelous fragrance; blooms late Feb.–Apr.	As wide as it is tall; grows also in southern Zone 5. Leaves hold well into Jan.; sometimes evergreen. Can be pruned to arching form.
Salix caprea French Pussy Willow	4–7	25	Fragrant silver-pink flowery catkins brushed with lemon stamens; late Mar.; branches can be forced earlier.	Broadly columnar, single-trunked small tree grew by my brook; new ones easily started from "whips" thrust into the bank. Handsomer than our native Feb.-blooming *S. discolor.* Thrives in damp or dry places; needs space and drastic pruning.
Sarcococca hookerana humilis Sweet Box	5–7	1½	Small white, fragrant flowers; blooms Feb.–Mar. Dark blue fruit.	Evergreen shrub; excellent for ground cover.

Spring Heath, see *Erica*
Spring Witch Hazel, see *Hamamelis*
Sweet Box, see *Sarcococca*
Winter Honeysuckle, see *Lonicera*
Winter Jasmine, see *Jasminum*
Wintersweet, see *Chimonanthus*

Less Reliable Shrubs Worth Trying

NAME	ZONE	HEIGHT IN FEET	DESCRIPTION AND FLOWERING TIME	COMMENTS
Daphne mezereum February Daphne	4–8	3	Magenta flowers fading to soft rose; 3 weeks of bloom from late Mar. on.	Not consistently reliable, but worth trying for fine scent; also white form 'Alba'. Best under high summer shade; berries poisonous. Set out young plants. *D. odora* extends to Zones 7 to 9, a delight in South.
February Daphne, see *Daphne* Fragrant Guelder, see *Viburnum* Japanese Apricot, see *Prunus* Leatherleaf Mahonia, see *Mahonia*				
Magnolia stellata Star Magnolia	5–9	15	Tree or shrub with marvelously fragrant, double white flowers, late Mar.	Not reliable about blooming; wet weather a hazard but a worthwhile possibility for many gardeners like me.
Mahonia bealei Leatherleaf Mahonia	6–9	3–12	Strings of scented yellow flowers; late Feb.–Mar. in good years. Evergreen plants.	For a protected place in partial shade; to 7' in South; prune to shapeliness.

Prunus mume Japanese Apricot	6–8	25	Marvelous fragrance from white flowers in propitious years; late Mar.	More tree than shrub; worth planting if you have space to experiment.
Star Magnolia, see *Magnolia*				
Viburnum farreri (*fragrans*) Fragrant Guelder	6–9	9	Lilac-scented rose-red-to-pink flowers; late Mar. before forsythia. Good for indoor forcing.	Upright shrub, may spread by suckers; needs protected place. Not always satisfactory except in southern range, but worth trying for earliness.

A planting of winter heather sets off a stone birdbath that won't crack in subzero weather. *Taloumis photo*

5

Invitation to the Winter Birds

BIRDS BRING LIFE and drama to the garden. Their subtle colors and graceful flights, their gay splashing and swift pursuits, are enchanting to watch, especially in winter when there is little competition for our concentration on flowers. To glimpse from my warm living room a bright red cardinal flying down from the cold snow-covered ledges beyond the garden fence, or a very blue jay noisily investigating the cones on ancient hemlocks in a snow flurry, is indeed heart-lifting. This cold-weather pleasure can readily be yours if you plan for it, and if your invitation to the birds is based on their needs and comfort. Except for a few species that naturally gather together in flocks, birds do not readily congregate in residential areas unless certain artificial means are used to tempt them. In suburban gardens particularly, where trees are not allowed to carry rotted limbs and there are no underbrush thickets, it takes a steadily maintained program to make birds feel enough at home to remain over winter.

Time and patience naturally enter into the matter, but so, too, does a determination to make the invitation to the birds irresistible by eliminating every unfriendly element. This is less trouble than at first appears, and pleasantly enough, the program is not dependent on the seasons but may be started at any time of year, even in late August or in September, to attract winter residents.

67

Indeed, it is surprising how many desirable birds will come to a garden and stay over winter if a food and water supply are made regularly available.

It's fun to keep a list of your winter birds. At a nearby nature center in Zone 6, fifty-one species have been recorded, although temperatures sometimes reach well below zero. More than two dozen species are likely to come to our gardens, including the Carolina wren and the southern mockingbird. These used to be rare in southern New England but now seem plentiful. Some cold day you might see, outside your "bird window," a field sparrow with its pink bill; the white-throated sparrow, its white napkin under its chin; and the song sparrow, its bow tie of brown distinguishing it from the ubiquitous English sparrow (really a finch), which is marked with a black four-in-hand and has a thicker neck. You will be amused by the white-breasted nuthatch miraculously eating upside-down at a suet stick, where later you can watch the hairy woodpecker eating right-side-up. The downy woodpecker may also be among those present—along with the brown creepers, chickadees, titmice, chewinks, maybe wrens and finches, red-breasted nuthatches, yellow-shafted flickers, and the myrtle warblers. Perhaps the far northern redpoll will visit your Norway spruce one very cold day. Or you will hear the beautiful gray mourning dove reiterate its wistful lament. Earlier you may have seen the cedar waxwing competently stripping your pyracantha of its bright berries, but he won't stay through winter; he is just getting a square meal on his way south.

To get the most out of all this excitement, you need a well-illustrated bird book to help you identify the individual visitors. A few of my favorite books are listed at the end of this chapter. The inexpensive government pamphlets are also excellent. Perhaps your Christmas list will include field glasses so that you can study your cold-weather visitors at long range from the comfort of your house.

Winter Feeding

Food for birds can be a simple matter, but some enthusiasts offer fare as varied as a hotel menu with raisins, shelled peanuts, and apple halves. Toast, crackers, and oranges are often acceptable dainties, but the commercial fare is both good and convenient. The seed-eating birds are well provided for by the natural fare found in your garden, particularly if a section can be left rather rough, if in addition a mixture of hemp, millet, sunflower seeds, and cracked corn (baby-chick size) is always at hand. You can buy such a mixture already packaged at most supermarkets, hardware stores, and garden centers.

If you offer the popular sunflower seeds alone, hoping to please cardinals among others (but only the lady cardinal comes here to a raised feeder), be prepared for an area of scratched-up turf below the feeder and also some unwanted "seedlings." One of my feeders hangs over a big stone beside an outdoor faucet, an area easily kept clean. I had to move another feeder because it appealed so much to blue jays that their wild cries kept guests awake in the bedroom above. And when a feeder was hung over my open terrace, I found myself supplying not only convention facilities but a comfort station. Terrace and walks required sweeping several times a day and considerable hard-spot cleaning as well. It was convenient to fill the feeder outside the terrace door but I moved it to quieter quarters with less housecleaning.

Seed eaters, such as song sparrows and juncos, naturally gather their food on or near the ground; consequently they will more readily find the food you provide if it is scattered there. But this is wasteful, especially in stormy winter weather, because the food gets soggy and unfit to eat. Since most birds readily learn new ways, some form of window-shelf or hanging feeder is practical in winter, with food scattered beneath it only until the birds learn about the supply above.

The fanciest receptacles for the grains will not always prove to be the most attractive. Where squirrels are not a problem, a shelf nailed to a sunny, out-of-the-wind spot will draw many birds, once they have learned its location. Fasten it to the side of a stump, the rail of a fence, or a windowsill; keep it constantly filled, and it won't be long before it will always be in need of refilling. A copper-roofed coconut-shell feeder suspended by a thin wire from high-branched trees will draw many visitors. Numerous other types of commercial feeders are available. I like my Satellite feeder that I fill with sunflower seed. This type is only for the "clingers"—chickadees, nuthatches, titmice, finches, and others—for it has no platform. But any feeder will do if it is made according to the principle that a proper one is a "weatherproof storehouse for a quantity of food where birds can get at it, other animals cannot." And this means out of the reach of squirrels or with a baffle protection on a pole-raised feeder. Squirrels can easily jump 10 feet.

Narrow, dark, blind-alley arrangements are to be avoided because birds fear to enter them. Hence the frequent use in popular feeders of a glass instead of a

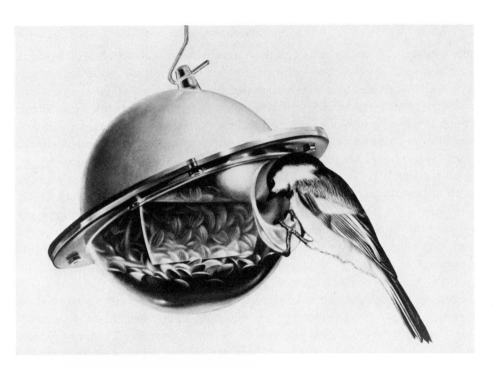

ABOVE: A Satellite bird-feeder for sunflower seeds alone delights chick-adees, nuthatches, titmice, flinches, and others. *James R. Waite, Inc., photo.* BELOW: After the nuthatch selects his seed from the feeder, he retires to this standard lilac tree to enjoy it. *Swinehart photo*

wood back, with height and depth of generous size, at least 12 by 12 inches square.

The *insect eaters*, such as the downy and hairy woodpeckers, chickadees, and nuthatches, are pleased by beef-kidney suet. Of course, some birds, like the chickadees, are not particular; they will eat seeds or insects. I like to watch a chickadee extract a sunflower seed from my Satellite feeder and retire to the standard lilac to deal with it. One device for providing suet is the suet food-stick. This can be made from a 20- to 24-inch section of any tree limb that has rough bark and is 2 to 4 inches in diameter. Bore twelve to fifteen holes in the stick, each hole ¾ inch in diameter and ¾ inch deep, and each sloping up at a slight angle, so that when the stick is hung upright from some branch or projection, water will not lodge in the holes and decay the wood. Press the suet into the holes and hang the stick (or sticks) where you can see it from a window, but where there is protection from cold winds. You will find you have to fill it more than once during the winter, for your invited birds must be steadily provided for. Metal stick-feeders are now available but are less attractive, I think, than the rough-bark type, although the latter can also sometimes be purchased in nature centers. I have a wire-mesh contraption suspended from a birdcage hanger that birds like, especially the small woodpeckers.

Water in Winter

Keeping a birdbath unfrozen in winter, and the vessel uncracked in zero weather, is a challenge. A weather-resistant pedestal birdbath is an attractive means of supplying water. It can also serve as an interesting garden accent and, because it is elevated, it is not submerged by snow. I had one such bath in the center of a small rose garden within clear view of the living room; more secluded, but still visible from the house, another such bath stood in the midst of hemlock and rhododendron. But water froze in both of them, and it took real devotion to go out and thaw them in freezing weather. I also set out a large flowerpot saucer close to the terrace door. The blue jays just fitted in for bathing but, alas, I discovered that a flowerpot saucer is not proof against zero weather. The vessel cracked. I thawed it daily before I realized that all the water was seeping out—as the ice melted, the saucer emptied.

I had to find other means, and in John K. Terres's book *Songbirds in Your*

Feeders for birds, on facing pages. These feeders hang or are supported by a pole, usually with a wide baffle to keep squirrels away. The narrow feeder, *lower left on this page*, has a dozen openings for "tidbits."

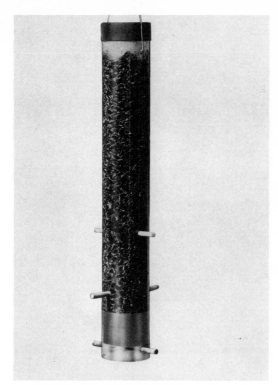

The tube feeder, *upper left*, has six openings made only for sunflower seeds, which are particularly attractive to cardinals. The nylon net bag holds suet seed-cakes, much relished by chickadees. *All photos Hyde's Inc.*

In a setting of English ivy, this stone water basin for birds decorates a city Japanese garden. *Taloumis photo*

Garden, I read of a simple device, a pan or saucer of water placed on top of a window-shelf feeder. This can be reached by opening the window. Thawing it indoors, refilling it with hot water once or twice a day, and replacing it through the window is an easier business than taking care of a birdbath outside the house. The birds love the steaming water as you will see when they come to it almost before you close your window.

A small immersion heater like those used in aquariums is another helpful device. Along this principle a water warmer, which automatically turns on and off at preset temperatures, is now on the market. It is fairly expensive but well worth the cost to those of us who are concerned about the comfort of our winter birds. (This water warmer is available from Hyde's Incorporated, the company that also supplies birdhouses. See "Where to Buy" at the end of this book.)

In any case, wherever low baths are set, it is important that the locations be open enough to be safe from cats. When its feathers are wet, a bird cannot fly far. Place the bath near a low tree or convenient shrub, but take care not to have

Birds are attracted to garden plants that, like this dill, carry seedheads through the winter. *Fitch photo*

this drying-room area so dense as to make a hiding place for prowling cats or other enemies that might pounce upon the bathers. A prickly shrub such as barberry or a Japanese rose is a good cat deterrent.

Trees, Shrubs, and Houses

You can make your place particularly attractive to winter birds by planting food-bearing trees and shrubs and by allowing some corner of your tidy property to include a thicket. Evergreens are also necessary for winter protection. Many berry-bearing shrubs offer cold-weather provisions for birds, and their favorites are noted in the chart of "Trees, Shrubs, and Vines with Winter Berries" at the end of the next chapter.

Protection from Enemies

Food, water, and shelter will not be sufficient enticement unless there is also ample protection, since birds will avoid gardens overrun by squirrels or frequently visited by cats. If there are a large number of squirrels, it may be necessary to trap some and turn them over to game wardens or nature centers. It all depends on the degree of protection afforded by the site in which the garden exists. Suspending feeders from fine wires drawn between two trees, so that the feeder is 10 feet from either tree, will usually keep squirrels away from food supplies. The surest method is to put a squirrel barrier on the support of a pole feeder. I had one feeder made with such a good baffle, an 18-inch-wide metal cone fastened just below the tray, that only one squirrel got in, in ten years. He must have been an abnormally gifted jumper, for this feeder stood supported by a 5-foot pole in an open area more than 10 feet from any tree.

Cats, of course, are deadly enemies and can make a bird program impossible, as mine once was when I had to be away for ten days. I asked a neighbor to keep the feeders full but she found them hardly ever used; in my absence, three neighborhood cats had invaded my garden, though they had never come near it when I was at home. If this is your unhappy lot, the only possible remedy is to request your neighbors to keep their cats at home or to bell them. (Politely asked, most neighbors are cooperative; mine have been.) Even bells don't always work, because some cats manage to get rid of their collars. (I have an idea a bell must give them nervous prostration!) However, for bird lovers like us, it's a sad thing to see cats stalking where the cardinals feed on the ground or hiding in the shrub thickets you have planted for the birds' protection.

But to return to the pleasure of bird companions, my winter day starts early with chickadees and titmice on the seed feeder, and a colony of juncos scratching in the garden, all making forays into the dogwood tree which surely has not a single morsel left. Consuming coffee and the *New York Times* at my kitchen window overlooking the small drama and with the view of the brilliant sun-streaked eastern sky, I think again that winter is my favorite season, and birds are one of its great joys.

For more information on this fascinating subject, send to the Superintendent of Documents, Government Printing Office, Washington, D.C. 20402, for several excellent leaflets by Chandler Robbins, Bertel Bruun, and Herbert S. Zin.

Attracting and Feeding Birds	$ .25
Fifty Birds of Town and City, cloth edition	4.00
paper edition	1.20
Invite Birds to Your Home—Midwest	.30
Invite Birds to Your Home—Northeast	.25
Song Birds	3.70

Among many other books, I particularly like *Birds of North America*, published by Golden Press, New York, N.Y. 10022. A great many birds are pictured and their range indicated in small maps beside each full-page color illustration. It is well bound in paper and priced at $4.95.

Fruits of the white snowberry, *Symphoricarpos albus*, which hang on in early winter, are effective in the garden in a setting of evergreens, and birds love them. *Genereux photo*

6

Bright Berries for the Garden, Food for the Birds

SMALL TREES AND SHRUBS THAT HOLD their fruits through the coldest months offer fine color accents for the winter garden, and also food for the birds whose bright plumage sparkles in the cold air. Birds like the gray berries of the bayberry, as well as the darker blue fruits of red cedar, privet, and hackberry. However, these do not provide color for the garden and so may have to be omitted, except on very large properties, in favor of the brightest plants. Sumac, though also red-berried and favored by many birds, is too coarse a plant except for extensive wild areas.

The choice of really handsome red-berried material for winter seems infinite. Some of it, like the dogwood, is fairly familiar. Much of it, especially among varieties of hawthorn, euonymus, holly, and viburnum, is less well known. In the charts at the end of this chapter are plants that make an undoubtedly stunning collection, since all have been chosen for brilliance, hardiness, and long-season color effect. Some, like the barberries, actually retain their berries until the next year's blossoms insist that they give way.

Aside from the sheer beauty of their fruit and the rich tones of early winter foliage, these are the trees and shrubs that attract the garden birds which devour the juicy fruits earlier in summer and fall, and the dried, somewhat bitter ones last. In mild winters the birds leave many of these for the gardener also to enjoy, but in seasons of snow and stress, when normal food supplies are cut down to about 2 percent, they will feast even upon the enduring fruit of the fire thorn.

In winter, in addition to berries, birds often feed on the "cones" of alders, birches, and sweet gums. When the wind strikes these, the seeds are blown out onto the ground to the delight of goldfinches and others. I like to see them worrying the tiny cones of the ancient hemlocks outside my windows. Woodpeckers, blue jays, and nuthatches come to my feeders, but they also eat the acorns of the pin oak. If you have a tall Colorado or Norway spruce, or a white or Scotch pine, on your place, you will very likely see the birds eating their seeds and also welcoming the shelter of the evergreen branches.

Trees with Berries

It is often difficult to label some plants *trees* and others *shrubs*. Many kinds can be treated either way. It all depends on pruning. The simplest distinction is that a woody plant grown with one trunk is a tree, while a shrub has several or many main stems. So, considering their usual manner of growth, I select among berried trees the Washington thorn, dogwood, American holly, another holly, *Ilex decidua* (the possum haw), and the glorious mountain ash.

In any garden of less than an acre, where trees are wanted principally for shade, one of these might be given room for its bright fruit, and then, perhaps, one or more of the shrubby types can be added. Most of these berried plants are dominant growers, strong, lusty, and wanting room; they are particularly handsome when allowed a free range for their talents. Hence satisfaction is greater when they are used as prominent specimens and allowed to develop a natural, unpruned shape. You will notice that the berried crops are usually heavier in alternate years.

The Washington thorn, *Crataegus cordata* or *phaenopyrum*, is an amazingly beautiful tree, especially when seen under a blue October sky, with its scarlet foliage a background for a tremendous abundance of large, shiny red corymbs of fruit. These persist colorfully even into March, being among the last to attract the birds, which prefer softer and juicier fruit. Native from Virginia to Alabama and Missouri, the Washington thorn is hardy in New York and Boston, too, where it eventually reaches a dignified 25 to 30 feet. If there is room for it, this

The Washington thorn, *Crataegus phaenopyrum*, is a handsome tree, spectacular in fruit—which lasts into winter, if robins and cedar waxwings do not strip it first—and glorious in autumn with scarlet foliage. *Taloumis photo*

Washington thorn may be grandly planted in a driveway or boundary row.

The flowering dogwood, *Cornus florida*, is the special treasure of Philadelphia and Valley Forge, where the plantings are unusually massive and lovely. In one of my own early gardens, I had a treasured pair of shapely specimens planted beside a brick entrance walk. At no season were they anything but commandingly beautiful. In October the foliage turned a gorgeous crimson and the shining

Red fruits of American holly, *Ilex opaca*, are bright all winter and attract many birds. *Taloumis photo*

berries studded the branches for weeks into early winter (the number of weeks depending on the appetites of the birds—and also on the appeal of the fruit to squirrels, who can clean up a crop in a few days). More than eighty-five kinds of birds, the records show, look on the glistening red dogwood berries as item number one on their favorite menus. I gladly shared my crop with robins, cardinals, and others, since the fruiting season is but one of the attractions of the dogwood. Native from Massachusetts to Florida, and west to Ontario and Texas, this dogwood seems to have everything.

The American holly, *Ilex opaca*, is another general favorite, although it is planted less often than it might be because of a misapprehension concerning its manner of fruiting. Since this holly is dioecious (that is, with male and female flowers on separate specimens), two specimens must be included in a planting to ensure berries. The female tree may be prominently planted and the male—lacking conspicuous fruits, and smaller perhaps, but still an attractive evergreen—may be inconspicuously placed in the shrubbery border.

From the standpoint of berries, American holly is particularly desirable, because its glory is a winter matter. An evergreen, it dots itself with red in late November and at Christmas time becomes the very symbol of the season. Move it any time from fall to spring when the ground is not frozen, but preferably in early fall when the young wood has almost ripened, or in the spring before growth starts. The ideal location for holly is a partially shaded spot with protection from west wind. The soil must be well drained, acid, and preferably sandy. A 3-inch mulch of peat moss is excellent, especially during the first year. Under such conditions the American holly will grow to 40 feet and endure with equanimity the rigors of even hard winters.

Ilex decidua is a gem of a small tree growing some 20 feet high. As the name indicates, it is not evergreen. Southern nurseries usually carry it, but in the North it is hard to find because it is considered tender—though this is not the case, since this holly has survived 17 degrees below zero in Philadelphia. Native from Virginia to Florida and west to Texas, *I. decidua*, thickly covered with large red fruits, suggests a cherry tree bearing its bright burden somewhat late in the season. Such is its form, although the bark is pale gray. It is definitely among the very finest of berried plants, beautiful enough to search for diligently. Self-pollinating, this holly is little trouble to grow and produces large, attractive fruit. Coming from swampy areas, it needs plenty of water.

The European mountain ash, or rowan, *Sorbus aucuparia*, fruiting early and hanging late, offers a treat from August to March, a display that pleases fifteen species of birds and every gardener. It varies from medium height to 45 feet, with pinnate leaves in most species, and is a commanding tree for any landscape. Fine hybrids have been developed with white, yellow, orange, or unusually large scarlet fruits.

The Bright Shrubs

Among the berried shrubs, there is another deciduous holly to consider, *Ilex verticillata*, the common winterberry or black alder. Native to eastern North America, from Nova Scotia to western Ontario and Missouri, it grows some 9 feet high and spreads to 15 feet, a superb plant at the height of its autumn grandeur. Like many hollies, it is dioecious, requiring both male and female plants for pollination. It is among our most adaptable natives, growing equally well in swampy or dry land, in sun or shade. Its shade tolerance is, of course, a valuable asset, since most of the berry-bearers demand the sun. The verticillata fruit is coral-red and thickly distributed along the stem. In October the yellow-green of the foliage turns bronze and really glimmers in the sun. In the Pennsylvania mountains it has earned the name fire bush. Birds do not immediately strip it as they may the dogwood, but by early winter the fire (fruit) is likely to be gone.

An attractive upright shrub for the edge of a woodland or the forefront of a mixed shrub border, the native red chokeberry, *Aronia arbutifolia*, offers a big crop of red berries that lasts well into winter, and if the planting is in the sun, the autumn foliage will turn a fine red to set off the crop of fruit.

The barberry family is famous for at least one variety, *Berberis thunbergii* or Japanese barberry. In trimmed hedges it will ever be pathetic to me, but planted either as a hedge or as a specimen where space is not limited and the pruning shears are withheld, it becomes something grand, with sparkling berries like ladies' earrings hanging in gay abundance from each blazing, foliaged branch. And these cling on to adorn the bare branches all winter long. Less familiar, and highly recommended, is the Korean barberry, *B. koreana*, handsome in foliage, in flower, and particularly in fruit, which also hangs in glowing clusters. The dense growth creates an impenetrable barrier.

Where a low plant is desirable, there is the rockspray, *Cotoneaster horizontalis*, one of two particularly handsome members of the cotoneaster group. It has flat, spraying branches, perfect for foaming over a low wall or hanging above a slope. It may even serve as a ground cover. Semievergreen in the North, evergreen and fruiting heavily in the South, this shrub endures hot, dry, sunny situations and puts on a beautiful September and October show by studding its branches thickly with a display of scarlet berries and orange-to-red foliage.

The red chokeberry, *Aronia arbutifolia*, produces lasting red berries as well as spectacular red autumn foliage. *Genereux photo*

The autumn olive, *Elaeagnus umbellatus*, grows to 12 feet, a spreading silvery bush with silvery red fruits that hang until February. Resembling the Russian olive, but a smaller shrub, this offers a pleasing color contrast, and twenty-five species of our birds enjoy the fruits. It grows well in moist-to-dry soil and in sun to light shade and is native to Zone 3.

The fire thorn, *Pyracantha coccinea,* especially the 'Lalandei' variety, is one of

Gorgeous orange-red berries make the fire thorn, *Pyracantha coccinea*, one of the most spectacular of winter shrubs. *Genereux photo*

the most magnificent of the fruiting shrubs. It looks to me like an autumn-leaf bonfire that has got a little out of hand and is burning madly on just to please itself. The heavily clustered fruit is orange with all the brilliance of flame, and it may remain into late January. The ultimate height of the shrub is 6 feet and the spread is to 10 feet; grown as a vine it may reach 8 feet in height. A well-grown specimen in the fruiting season is indeed a grand sight, but whether the birds will strip it early of its ornaments is a question. The claim is made for a September-to-March display in some areas that seventeen species of birds enjoy.

The shrubby *Rosa rugosa* produces large orange-red fruit called "hips" and thick growth that offers winter protection for birds. *Genereux photo*

Two shrub roses, *Rosa multiflora* and *R. rugosa*, are tall, "rough," spreading plants to grow outside the garden proper. I have enjoyed these plants set along the far side of a post-and-rail fence. The large and numerous panicles of small white flowers of *R. multiflora* have a rampant and "wild" character unlike other roses; and the purple-red blooms of the rugosas open over a long period. The "hips," as the orange-red fruits are called, delight the birds. The dense growth of these species of roses offers winter protection as well as food and nesting sites in spring. These shrub roses grow well at the seashore. Today there are many hybrids and named varieties, with summer-blooming flowers in various tints of pink, crimson, yellow, and white; the habit of shrubby, thorny, year-round growth is invaluable.

The Japanese skimmia has proved far hardier for me in Zone 6, where the temperature only occasionally falls below zero, than is generally claimed. Broader than it is high, this 4-foot shrub produces fragrant spring flowers followed by clusters of scarlet berries that do not appeal to the birds until most other supplies are exhausted late in winter. Both male and female plants are required for fruiting, the male grown in an inconspicuous spot. I grew skimmias successfully in a somewhat shaded, northeastern location inside a stone wall that protected them from wind. If the temperature in your garden does not go below zero, the spectacular berried skimmia will be fairly safe and a handsome addition to your winter garden. You might plant the female shrubs for bright effect in front of the tall rhododendrons or azaleas that also require a somewhat acid soil and a good mulch. Another species, of recent introduction, *S. reevesiana*, grows to somewhat less height, is hardy to Zone 7, and bears perfect flowers, hence will be fertilized and produce fruits. The leaves are dull green but the berries are prolific in the fall and, in sheltered places, last even into January.

One shrub with white fruits, the snowberry, *Symphoricarpos albus*, is a

The bitter berries of the evergreen *Skimmia japonica* are left till last by the birds. (This male plant carries flower buds through winter; the female clones have clusters of red berries.) *Fitch photo*

treasure to lighten a shaded area. It is low-growing and excellent for the front of the shrub border where this passes out of the sun; the snowberry shows up well in early winter when the leaves have fallen and the white berries are silhouetted against the dark green of hemlocks or against a group of taller broad-leaved shrubs like mountain laurel or Japanese andromeda. I am glad to see that nurserymen are offering snowberries again.

Although the viburnum family is chiefly famous because it contains the common snowball, it includes far more distinguished members. The high-bush cranberry, *Viburnum trilobum* or *americanum*, has long pleased both me and the birds. Extremely hardy even to Zone 2, this spreading native shrub offers clusters of bright red fruits all through winter. So, too, does the European cranberry, *V. opulus*, with vivid red, bitter berries that become transparent and also stay through winter.

LEFT: The clusters of glossy scarlet berries that hang on through winter on the American cranberry bush, *Viburnum trilobum*, are food for some thirty-four species of birds. RIGHT: The Japanese dogwood, *Cornus kousa*, produces fleshy pink-red fruits and offers safe winter cover. *Genereux photos*

The waxy gray berries of the semievergreen aromatic bayberry shrub, *Myrica pensylvanica*, are favored by more than seventy species of birds. *Genereux photo*

Fruiting Vines

Four handsome vines produce winter-long berries but all four are for special situations. I grow the evergreen (really semievergreen) bittersweet, *Euonymus fortunei*, against the divider on the south side, also along the picket fence. This small-leaved vine grows to 6 feet fairly quickly here, but must reach greater ma-

The dark red berries of the spectacular staghorn sumac, *Rhus typhina*, last from September to May, to the delight of seventeen species of birds. *Fitch photo*

turity before it produces berries for a late-winter meal for the birds. It is one of the most attractive of the evergreen vines. (In the same family, *E. patens* is not a vine but a grand hedge plant and fruits only in the South; *E. sachalinensis* is a great spreading semievergreen shrub with bright red fuchsialike flowers, effective where there is space for it.)

The deciduous American bittersweet, *Celastrus scandens*, is a familiar sight in woodlands and planted along roadsides. I see it climbing evergreens along the Merritt Parkway, its colorful orange berries making a glorious red-and-green harmony on cedars, pines, and hemlocks. But this vine is not to be planted except where there is plenty of room, for it can be a nuisance despite its beauty. It requires as much space for its width as for its 20-foot height; if you have a gaunt, dead tree on your place, drape it with this bittersweet for a beautiful picture.

The Virginia creeper or woodbine, *Parthenocissus quinquefolia*, and Boston ivy, *P. tricuspidata*, are for house walls or old stone fences. Both have dark blue berries that have the advantage of hanging on through winter and appealing to many birds, but neither has the garden appeal of a red-berried shrub.

For the winter garden, trees and shrubs with bright berries are a fine sight, particularly in association with evergreens—and a nice light fall of snow. Plant your berry-bearers in good view of the house, where you can watch the birds enjoying the fruits. In time, Virginia creeper and Boston ivy will completely enframe the windows of a brick house, and thrushes, robins, finches, and sparrows can often be plainly seen resting or pausing on the windowsill.

You can see in the chart that follows what wealth of attractive berried material you can select to decorate your yard or garden. You may have room for only one tree and, perhaps, three or four of these shrubs, for most of them require considerable space, but these are all plants that add to the beauty of the winter landscape as they attract the birds that in winter are colorful substitutes for the flowers of summer.

Trees, Shrubs, and Vines with Winter Berries

The length of time these plants hold their berries varies with their location, the weather, and the onslaught of the birds in some seasons. A flock may arrive to strip a plant one year and leave the berries on the same plant until spring another year. In the cross-references the most familiar common name is used, as Privet instead of Regel Privet.

NAME	ZONE	HEIGHT IN FEET	BERRIES FOR BIRDS	COMMENTS
Aronia arbutifolia Red Chokeberry	4–9	9	Small, effective white flowers in spring; abundant fall crop of red berries lasting well into winter; spectacular red autumn foliage.	For moist or dry soil in light to deep shade; large, native shrub of irregular form.
Autumn Olive, see *Elaeagnus* Barberry, see *Berberis* Bayberry, see *Myrica*				
Berberis koreana Korean Barberry	4–9	4	Yellow flowers in mid-May; red autumn foliage, with pendent clusters of brilliant orange-red fruits that color in fall and hang on well into winter.	Thorny twigs; deciduous shrub with spreading, arching growth. A good substitute for *B. vulgaris*, which carries wheat rust.
B. thunbergii Japanese Barberry	4–9	4–5	Small white flowers in spring; berries strung along stems last through winter longer than those of any other shrub; scarlet autumn foliage.	Endures deep shade, dry soil; makes a prickly barrier or bank plant for sun or shade. Dependable even in worst situations. Variety 'Minor' is 12″ to 18″ with dense growth; good for low, red hedge.

93

NAME	ZONE	HEIGHT IN FEET	BERRIES FOR BIRDS	COMMENTS
Bittersweet, see *Celastrus* Black Alder, see *Ilex* Boston Ivy, see *Parthenocissus* Cedar, see *Juniperus*				
Celastrus scandens American Bittersweet	2–8	to 25	Colorful orange berries in early fall may hang through winter; only female vines bear fruit, male pollinator required.	Not for the small garden but a grand wanderer where there is space for wild, dense hedging or a dead tree to climb and decorate with brilliant fruit display. For sun or shade. 'Loesneri' has both male and female flowers on same plant; yellow-to-orange berries.
Celtis occidentalis Hackberry	3–7	80	High, branching tree with seedy blue berries favored by at least 35 bird species.	Berries persist through fall, winter, and spring. Not for small properties.
Cornus florida Flowering Dogwood	4–9	25	Shiny red berries sought by 85 species through fall and early winter. Sometimes squirrels get there first. Crimson autumn foliage.	Handsome small tree with horizontal branches for open lawn or in the shade of other trees where there is shifting sunlight. Prune flat or let droop gracefully toward the ground. Needs deep watering in drought.

C. kousa Japanese Dogwood	5–8	20	Smaller dogwood with fleshy pink-red fruits resembling strawberries; nice to have both dogwoods.	Bushy growth, very shade-tolerant; blooms 3 weeks after *C. florida*.
Cotoneaster horizontalis Rockspray	4–9	3	June flowers followed by red fruits; more prolific in warm areas; semi-evergreen.	Horizontal branching makes this valuable for foaming over walls, training as an espalier, or use as ground cover.
Crab Apple, see *Malus* Cranberry Bush, see *Viburnum*				
Crataegus cordata (phaenopyrum) Washington Thorn	4–8	25	Rounded thorny native tree with red berries to please 33 species in winter if robins and cedar wax-wings do not strip tree first; scarlet autumn foliage.	One of the last hawthorns to bloom; more spectacular in winter fruit than in spring flower. Fruit so heavy it looks like a second blooming. Avoid proximity to junipers because of rust. Deep rooting; tolerates shade. Good city tree.
Dogwood, see *Cornus*				
Elaeagnus umbellatus Autumn Olive	3–9	12	Fruits scarlet, silvery when young; Sept.–Feb., used by 25 species.	Silvery foliage on a large spreading bush; small yellow fragrant flowers, May–June.

NAME	ZONE	HEIGHT IN FEET	BERRIES FOR BIRDS	COMMENTS
Euonymus fortunei 'Vegeta' Evergreen Bittersweet	5–9	20	Bright orange fruits often in good condition from winter into spring; birds finally eat them.	Really semievergreen; can be trained as vine or left unpruned as a shrub that piles up its horizontal branches. Plant all in semishade to avoid scale.
E. kiautschovica (patens) Spreading Euonymus	6–9	7	Green-white flowers; early Sept. in South; late pinkish or red fruits where growing season long enough.	Handsome spreading evergreen for North but without fruits there. Good hedge plant.
E. sachalinensis (planipes)	5–8	12	Bright crimson fall leaves; large, pendent bright red fruits like fuchsia flowers hang in profusion on into winter.	From northeast Asia and Japan, a semievergreen shrub spreading to 12'. Interesting for unusual and abundant fruits.
Evergreen Bittersweet, see *Euonymus* Fire Thorn, see *Pyracantha* Hackberry, see *Celtis* Holly, see *Ilex*				
Ilex decidua Possum Haw	5–8	20	Bright orange-red berries held well into winter, often longer.	Southeastern native deciduous tree with lustrous foliage. Self-pollinating; needs plenty of water.

Name			Description
I. opaca American Holly	5–9	40	Favorite with 45 species for red berries well into Feb. and dense protective foliage.	Spectacular native evergreen tree, bushy or pyramidal. Male tree is essential for pollination but can be small and unimportantly placed. Hollies endure quite damp situations and prefer partial shade.
I. verticillata Winterberry or Black Alder	3–9	9	Large deciduous holly. Bright red berries for early winter for 22 species.	A shrub with a 15′ spread. Best in acid soil. Also a dwarf variety to 3′ tall with very large berries.
Japanese Dogwood, see *Cornus* Japanese Rose, see *Rosa multiflora*				
Juniperus virginiana 'Canaertii' Red Cedar	2–9	10	Abundance of bluish berries and dense, dark green foliage supply both food and winter cover for 39 species throughout the winter.	Pyramidal, slow-growing form of native red cedar; excellent specimen for full sun, drought-tolerant. Makes a good evergreen hedge, but not as effective in winter garden as red-berried shrubs, except as back-line for small gardens.
Ligustrum obtusifolium regelianum Regel Privet	3–8	4–5	Most graceful of privets; birds delight in the blue-black berries and winter protection of twiggy horizontal branches.	Small glossy leaves; plants withstand city conditions; hardy in light, not deep, shade.

NAME	ZONE	HEIGHT IN FEET	BERRIES FOR BIRDS	COMMENTS
Malus 'Dorothea' Crab Apple	4–8	25	Semidouble pink flowers in May; yellow fruits from fall to early winter.	One of very few double-flower crab apples to produce ornamental fruit; attractive tree for small property.
Mountain Ash, see *Sorbus*				
Myrica pensylvanica Bayberry	2–8	6	Abundance of waxy, gray berries favored by at least 73 species.	Rangy, semievergreen shrub, aromatic foliage; for light or deep shade; tolerates poor soil, some dampness; good for seacoast.
Parthenocissus quinquefolia Virginia Creeper or Woodbine	3–8	50	Rambling native vine with fine fall color and a wealth of blue-black berries that hang on to Feb. for 37 species.	Vines usually grown on house walls but also makes pleasing covering for New England stone fences; has 5 large leaflets.
P. tricuspidata Boston Ivy	4–8	50	Glowing scarlet autumn foliage; dark blue fruit hardly visible until leaves fall, then decorative until late winter.	Boston ivy has 3 leaflets (same as poison ivy); not to grow against wood. Will reach the top of a 3-story house. Birds may nest in the woody growth.
Possum Haw, see *Ilex*				

Privet, see *Ligustrum*

Pyracantha coccinea Fire Thorn	5–8	6–8	Inconspicuous but charming white spring flowers; gorgeous orange-red berries all winter unless stripped early; enjoyed by 17 species.	Grown as a broad shrub or tall trellised vine; needs full sun or early morning sun, protected location; almost evergreen. 'Lalandei' choice variety.

Red Chokeberry, see *Aronia*

Rhus typhina Staghorn Sumac	3–8	15	Heads of dark red berries delight some 93 species and last Sept.–May.	Not for limited areas; coarse but spectacular for a grove. Stiff not graceful growth.

Rockspray, see *Cotoneaster*

Rosa multiflora Japanese Rose	5–8	8	Very bushy, small-leaved. Small abundant red fruits; not too hardy in very cold winters.	Wildly rampant, not for a limited area; can be trained as a vine or living fence or let ramble as high ground cover; endures some shade.
R. rugosa Rugosa Rose	3–8	5–8	Dense, spreading with a wealth of orange-red fruit, called "hips," that birds flock to; thick growth makes fine winter protection and nesting sites. Well suited to seashore conditions.	Long season; purple-red blooms and cultivars with white, pink, and yellow flowers. 'Frau Dagmar Hartopp', a smaller white-flowering plant, also produces rose hips that please the birds.

NAME	ZONE	HEIGHT IN FEET	BERRIES FOR BIRDS	COMMENTS
Rose, see *Rosa*				
Rowan, see *Sorbus*				
Skimmia japonica Japanese Skimmia	7–8	4	Fragrant white flowers in spring; bright red berries, bitter-tasting, left by birds till last.	Handsome evergreen; male pollinator necessary for fruiting. Hardy for me in Zone 6, grown next to a protecting stone wall.
Snowberry, see *Symphoricarpos*				
Sorbus aucuparia European Mountain Ash or Rowan	2–7	45	Flat white flower clusters in May–June; glowing bright-red-to-orange berries Aug.–Feb.; 15 species enjoy them.	Handsome tree for moist to dry soil in sun. One of the most outstanding of fruiting ornamentals.
Sumac, see *Rhus*				
Symphoricarpos albus laevigatus Snowberry	3–9	2–5	White-berried shrub effective in front of evergreens or other tall plants; large fruits last into winter and are favored by 25 species.	Makes a good thicket in deep shade; may bend to ground when weighted by fruit; thrives in dry soil. 'Mother of Pearl' hybrid with pink berries.

Viburnum opulus European Cranberry Bush	3–7	12	Dense growth; orange-to-red autumn leaves; vivid red, bitter berries that become transparent as they stay on through winter.	Effective massed for color of white May flower and red fruits; stands dryness and heat. 'Compactum' to 5'; 'Xanthocarpum' with yellow fruits.
V. trilobum (americanum) American Cranberry Bush or High-Bush Cranberry	2–5	10	Spreading native shrub with clusters of glossy scarlet berries that hang on through winter; food for 34 species.	More cold-tolerant than most viburnums. Effective winter shrub especially in snow. Oval berries first yellow on one side, red on the other, then all red.

Virginia Creeper, see *Parthenocissus*
Washington Thorn, see *Crataegus*
Winterberry, see *Ilex*
Woodbine, see *Parthenocissus*

A light covering of snow enhances the shapely form of this Siberian crab apple, *Malus baccata*, which casts such a beautiful shadow. A tree lilac rises in the background. *Taloumis photo*

7

Forms and Traceries of Deciduous Trees

THE BEAUTY OF OUR WINTER WORLD is wonderfully enhanced by the dry-point etchings of the deciduous trees. Their great variety of forms and traceries is now excitingly presented, for without their burden of leaves, they offer us a wealth of new pictures. Indeed, we cannot completely know our trees until we have experienced their fourth-season beauty. Until we have closely observed them in their cold-winter stillness, we may not have been aware of so many differences of forms—tall, broad oaks and beeches; narrow, slender birches; oval sugar maples; wide-spreading maidenhair trees; and the charmingly pendent willows. Now, with leafy distractions gone, we notice perhaps for the first time the fascinating peculiarities of bark. In some trees, like the buttonwood or plane tree, the Chinese elm, and the paperbark maple, it flakes off or exfoliates in irregular sections; bark is furrowed in the sweet gum and tulip tree. The cucumber tree and saucer magnolia have gray bark; the Sargent cherry is dark red to brown; and the paperbark maple is cherry-red. And I must mention here an evergreen, the lace-bark pine, *Pinus bungeana*, whose bark peels off in large irregular patches to show the new, smooth, bluish-white bark beneath.

What you *see* in your winter view can be much more than what you simply

The European weeping beech, *Fagus sylvatica*, makes a handsome specimen where there is adequate space for its development. *Taloumis photo*

look at. Once the leaves have fallen, new outdoor pictures appear. From the back of my house I look through the bare trunks and high-up branches of ancient hemlocks, themselves like a Japanese print, to a handsome white birch tree—a canoe birch 60 feet tall with three lofty trunks. Beside it a Japanese maple stretches out its branches to make a natural study of the perpendicular and the horizontal. These smaller maples—and there are a number of kinds,

The glistening white bark of the tall European birch, *Betula pendula*, is harmonious in this all-white winter scene. *Taloumis photo*

as the Amur maple and the vase-shaped Nikko—are just as interesting in winter as they are beautiful in summer, and, of course, they are particularly well suited to our smaller properties because of their own smaller scale. Beyond this arresting view, a giant sugar maple, perhaps 100 feet in the air, guards the country road and in all seasons is glorious from my study window.

This four-trunked paper birch, *Betula papyrifera*, with the whitest bark of all the birches, makes a handsome specimen lawn tree. *Taloumis photo*

I also like to see an interesting tree form when I open my front door. On the terrace of my town house rises a graceful, well-pruned honey locust, its winter frame etched against the sky, as pleasing to me as its earlier feathery foliage. When I lived in the country, a beautifully shaped fringe tree grew by my front steps, its well-balanced structure in the fourth season as attractive to me as when, in full bloom, its white tassels took the breeze.

Oddly enough, a few deciduous trees hold their leaves almost till spring and so add color to our winter view. The American beech is notably tenacious.

Well-pruned deciduous trees opposite front doors. LEFT: A young honey locust, *Gleditsia triacanthos*, rises on the terrace of my town house. RIGHT: An old open-pruned fringe tree, *Chionanthus virginicus*, arches above Stony Brook Cottage. *Swinehart and Taloumis photos*

In a winter woodland its gold-bronze foliage shines out among the leafless branches of other trees. This beech, with its smooth gray bark, is too large for most properties. However, it is a tree to "see" and enjoy for its color wherever it is found, alone or in groves (as I enjoyed it one cold, snowy day while driving through a great stretch of well-cared-for woodland).

The same day I beheld (you cannot simply view such a sight) an absolute giant of a European beech. This handsome tree—with its gray, many-trunked form—had been wisely respected by the builder of a condominium, who had placed the town houses so as to feature the tree for the pleasure of those who would live close by. Again, this beech is not for limited areas, but what a pleasure

Four studies in exfoliating bark. ABOVE LEFT: Canoe birch, *Betula papyrifera*. RIGHT: *Stewartia koreana*. BELOW LEFT: Paperbark maple, *Acer griseum*. RIGHT: Buttonwood, *Platanus occidentalis*. *Taloumis photos*

it is to dwell upon such an ancient specimen in its many-branched splendor, leafless and emphatic.

A few oaks offer leaf color, though it is not brilliant, into the winter. The white oak, *Quercus alba*, so-called for its pale trunk, and one of our truly magnificent trees, has large leaves that turn russet in late fall and gradually turn to a browner tone until February. The pin oak, *Q. palustris*, of most graceful pendent silhouette, has narrow, many-lobed, deep crimson leaves until December, when they turn brown and fall. The northern red oak, *Q. rubra*, colors its leaves dark red to red-brown in autumn, and they hang on for weeks.

Once you begin to see trees, all sorts of arresting pictures will delight, even amuse, you. Looking through the big windows of my daughter's house, across the lawn, I saw some ancient trees along a brook, a trio of giants I had not particularly noticed before. On the right was a three-pronged contorted ash, its left-hand trunk forming a terminal curlicue that was almost comic. In the center, an elegant swamp maple was shaped like a lady's long-handled fan, for it branched widely but loftily. Completing the trio, a gaunt, white-barked buttonwood shot up higher than either of the other two and tossed its sparse branches arrogantly in the winter air. So it is that in winter we can enjoy the new pictures that deciduous trees make.

If you are just planting a property, what opportunity you have to develop winter beauty in your near view! Perhaps some favorite trees will be almost too big for your area—I think of the American beech, the sugar maple, and the white oak, all growing 90 feet or higher—but you can probably have one such large tree if it can be wisely placed near the far boundary of your place. Then there are the medium growers—these are not giants but are in the eventual 60-foot range—like the green ash, yellow-wood, and American larch. Smaller trees that grow under 40 feet—such as the crab apple, dogwood, fringe tree, mountain ash, serviceberry, and silver-bell—may suit your property better. Also, some of the giants, like the tulip tree, grow so slowly that one would not outgrow you in, say, fifty years, although its ultimate height could be 125 feet. I would always have to have a tulip tree. You, too, will have favorites and you may want to develop an attractive association or two—such as the familiar 25-foot gray birch, really white, with hemlocks; or one or two 25-foot dog-woods with a white pine.

Also essential for me is a weeping tree. Many of the upright growers, such as the hawthorns and crab apples, have pendent forms. The classic is, of course, the Babylon weeping willow, but this is not so hardy or so pretty as the golden

The bizarre corkscrew willow, *Salix matsudana* 'Tortuosa', dominates this small pebble-strewn garden with its oriental air. *Taloumis photo*

weeping willow with its yellow bark that excites me in winter. All of these must be planted at least 50 feet from your house or you will have sewer problems. Furthermore, you may consider none of these willows a proper lawn tree, since constant cleanup of broken twigs, pods, and dried leaves is required. The Chinese elm, the European white birch, the 'Red Jade' crab apple, and the weeping Higan cherry or *Prunus subhirtella* 'Pendula' are other lovely possibilities.

As you become aware of trees and their many variations, you will probably want many more for your place than it can properly accommodate. So be thoughtful and selective. Trees in all seasons, but particularly in winter, are a most important aspect of your garden or planted place. Have a good idea of what you favor before you order. The following charts of large and small trees

Traceries and shadows of deciduous trees. TOP LEFT: *Malus* 'Dorothea', a shapely crab apple, casts a charming shadow on the snowy ground. TOP RIGHT: The tall *Magnolia soulangiana* has lofty winter beauty. ABOVE LEFT: The seed pods of the standard dwarf Korean tree lilac, *Syringa velutina*, produce an interesting winter picture. *Taloumis photos.* ABOVE RIGHT: In the wild, the silhouette of a sour-cherry tree, *Prunus cerasus*, is a dramatic accent. *Fitch photo*

can guide you, but only to a degree. You need to get acquainted with trees before you make any selections. Because you will value your trees for more than their winter beauty, their year-round appearance is also described in these charts.

Tall Deciduous Trees for Winter Beauty

Beech, the Norway and some other maples, poplars, and willows are not suggested here for lawn trees because they are shallow-rooted; neither lawns nor flower beds are likely to thrive beneath them. The trees listed here have year-round beauty and noteworthy winter forms.

NAME	ZONE	HEIGHT IN FEET	GROWTH	SHAPE	REMARKS
Acer saccharum Sugar Maple	3–6	90–100	Allow 50' to 60' space; slow to moderate growth; won't endure pollution.	Oval to round top; gray bark; fairly deep-rooted; broad-leaved shrubs and myrtle thrive under it.	Yellow, orange, scarlet fall coloring is the glory of New England. Remove branches 12' to 15' above ground.
Ash, see *Fraxinus*					
Betula papyrifera Canoe or Paper Birch	2–6	90	Grows fast; has whitest bark of all the birches.	Narrow, rounded at top.	Most popular birch because not so susceptible to borers.
B. pendula European Weeping White Birch	2–7	60	Grows fairly fast; fine white, black-barred trunk; choice lawn tree; allow 25' spread.	Conical form; deep-rooted, with graceful, drooping lateral branches; smaller leaves than canoe birch, same golden autumn color.	This can be pruned open for view of paths and plantings beyond. Cutleaf weeping birch 'Gracilis' also lovely.
Birch, see *Betula*					

NAME	ZONE	HEIGHT IN FEET	GROWTH	SHAPE	REMARKS
Cercidiphyllum japonicum Katsura Tree	4–7	60–100	Fast, good for tall screening at edge of property instead of Lombardy poplar; rather shallow-rooted, not for main lawn area.	Several trunks or pruned to one; needs rich, moist soil.	Fine-textured foliage; pink tint to unfolding leaves, scarlet and gold in autumn.

Chinese Scholar Tree, see *Sophora*

NAME	ZONE	HEIGHT IN FEET	GROWTH	SHAPE	REMARKS
Cladrastis lutea Yellow-wood	3–9	50–60	Allow 30' to 40' space. Medium-fast grower. Deep-rooted, tolerant of poor soil; a choice tree. Move carefully in spring with root ball.	Round-topped, spreading, low-branched. Prune midsummer to fall, not spring; a bleeder.	Lovely native with fragrant white flowers like wisteria in spring; orange-yellow autumn foliage; gray bark.

Dawn Redwood, see *Metasequoia*

NAME	ZONE	HEIGHT IN FEET	GROWTH	SHAPE	REMARKS
Fraxinus pennsylvanica lanceolata Green Ash	2–9	60	Fast-growing; leafs out late and leaves fall late.	Irregularly oval; grass grows well beneath it; good yellow autumn color; native, lovely on a lawn.	Plant pyramidal 'Marshall's Seedless' to avoid seed nuisance.

Ginkgo biloba Maidenhair Tree	4–9	100	Slow-growing.	Open, wide-spreading; fan-shaped leaves give lacy effect.	Makes a beautiful specimen; be sure of a male tree, very smelly fruits on females; brilliant yellow in fall.
Gleditsia triacanthos Honey Locust	4–9	125	Fast, among the very best.	High and open, gives light ferny shade; flowers and grass thrive beneath it; no autumn color; a very fine native tree.	Good for almost immediate effect. Select the thornless 'Inermis', 'Moraine', or 'Sunburst', with golden young leaves as if in bloom; casts beautiful winter shadows.

Green Ash, see *Fraxinus*

Halesia monticola Great Silver-Bell	5–9	70	Good in sun or semishade, in acid soil.	Short trunk and broad crown.	Can be grown with multiple trunks. Golden autumn coloring; nutlike fruits; large flowers.

Honey Locust, see *Gleditsia*
Katsura Tree, see *Cercidiphyllum*
Larch, see *Larix*

NAME	ZONE	HEIGHT IN FEET	GROWTH	SHAPE	REMARKS
Larix decidua European Larch	2–6	90	Fast, for well-drained soils.	Pyramidal in youth, spreading in age as branches droop.	Choice deciduous cone-bearer with a golden flame of needles in autumn before they drop; for edge of lawn, not center.
L. laricina American Larch or Tamarack	2–4	60	Fast, for moist to wet soils.	Pyramidal and pendent; native.	Notable hardiness even across northern Canada; common in New England marshy places; not so handsome as European.
Lime, see Tilia Linden, see Tilia					
Liquidambar styraciflua Sweet Gum	5–9	125	Moderate.	Broadly pyramidal; grass grows under it. Eastern native.	Star-shaped leaves, glorious crimson autumn color; globular, spiny fruits for Christmas decorations.

Liriodendron tulipifera Tulip Tree	4–7	125	Slow.	Wide branching flowers like dull yellow tulips in June; yellow autumn leaves.	Native to eastern states; most desirable.
Maidenhair Tree, see *Ginkgo* Maple, see *Acer*					
Metasequoia glyptostroboides Dawn Redwood	5–8	100	Fast; prune away side branches to 8' or 9'; allow 30' spread.	Pyramidal; needs big planting hole; can be transplanted bare root.	Deep-rooted; has amber autumn color; a rare deciduous cone-bearer but easy to grow.
Oak, see *Quercus* Pagoda Tree, see *Sophora*					
Quercus alba White Oak	4–8	100	Slow, with dense foliage; allow 60' to 70' space.	Rounded, spreading; a noble tree, native. Q. *bicolor* is the swamp white oak.	Deep-rooted. Acorns attract birds; dark purplish-red fall foliage.
Q. palustris Pin Oak	4–7	75	Moderate; can spread to 35'.	Pyramidal, low branches drooping to ground; fine native specimen.	Fairly deep-rooted; brilliant red in fall; must be pruned high for a lawn tree.

NAME	ZONE	HEIGHT IN FEET	GROWTH	SHAPE	REMARKS
Q. rubra Red Oak	3–7	75	Fast and spreading; allow 50'.	Rounded; deep-rooted; native.	Dark red fall foliage; not for small area.
Salix alba tristis Golden Weeping Willow	2–9	65	Very fast, can become major feature of a garden within 4 years and put everything around it out of scale.	Gracefully pendent. Branches are bright yellow, lovely. Needs regular pruning.	Not for planting within 50' of house; surface roots travel far, interfere with drains. Offers lovely contrasting texture and form; choice in *proper* place.
S. babylonica Weeping Willow	6–9	30–50	Fast.		
Sophora japonica Pagoda Tree or Scholar Tree	4–7	75	Needs 40' spread; slow to medium; won't tolerate wet, sour soil.	Round-topped, deep-rooted; plant away from terrace or steps because of flower and fruit litter.	Creamy pealike flower cluster in Aug.; evergreen effect in winter due to green bark and twig color; stands pollution; grass will grow under it.

Sweet Gum, see *Liquidambar*
Tamarack, see *Larix*

Tilia cordata Littleleaf Linden or Lime Tree	3–7	100	Slow; casts deep shade.	Symmetrical; pale yellow blooms in June–July are scented, particularly in early evening. Delicate, pendent branches, reddish in midwinter sunlight.	Small, heart-shaped leaves give nice texture effect to this European tree; endures pollution; favorite of aphids so don't plant next to terrace.
Tulip Tree, see *Liriodendron* Weeping Willow, see *Salix* Yellow-wood, see *Cladrastis*					
Zelkova serrata Japanese Zelkova	5–8	100	Fast; many slender ascending branches.	Rounded top, short trunk; prune to avoid too-thick growth.	This elm relative with lacy foliage replaces American elm; lovely fall coloring yellow to bronze; a charming tree.

Smaller Deciduous Trees

Select these for smaller properties, probably space for several.

NAME	ZONE	HEIGHT IN FEET	FLOWERS, FRUITS, FOLIAGE	SHAPE AND CULTURE	REMARKS
Acer ginnala Amur Maple	2–7	20	Red-winged seeds among green, hand-like leaves in late summer; yellow and vermilion fall colors.	Rounded. Very hardy.	One of the best small maples. Needs copious water in warm summers or leaves will yellow and brown.
A. nikoense (maximowiczianum) Nikko Maple	5–7	30	Scarlet autumn foliage.	Vase-shaped or round-topped.	From Japan; good for small property.
A. palmatum 'Atropurpureum' Japanese Maple	5–8	20	Holds red leaves through growing season.	Single or multiple trunks; flat branching shrub or tree. Partial shade, good soil, not dry.	Excellent specimen and one of hardiest.
Amelanchier canadensis Shadbush or Serviceberry	4–7	25	Single white Apr.–May flowers bloom before leaves; red berries in early summer soon stripped by birds.	Rounded-topped, slender tree. Sun and moist soil; plant away from junipers.	Fine native; yellow-to-red fall foliage is spectacular; also gray bark in winter.

Name					
Betula populifolia Gray Birch (but often called White)	4–6	25	Leaves turn to pure gold early in fall; common throughout Northeast.	Endures poor or rocky soils; here not so short-lived as claimed, but requires protection from leaf miner.	Lovely, graceful, white-barked accents to mark paths or contrast with hemlocks; select 3- or 4-pronged clumps; choice landscape tree throughout the year.
Birch, see *Betula* Black Alder, see *Ilex*					
Cercis canadensis Eastern Redbud or Judas Tree	4–9	30	Purple-pink flowers Apr.–May before leaves; brilliant yellow autumn foliage.	Growth flat at top. Sun or high shade.	Native from New England to Florida, same range as white dogwood; the two are good garden companions.
Cherry, see *Prunus*					
Chionanthus virginicus Fringe Tree	4–9	25	Silken white panicles in June; last to leaf out; marvelously fragrant.	Good with multiple trunks; can be pruned to suit site. Sun and good drainage.	Utterly beautiful, much too infrequently planted; lovely close to house but not next to walk or porch because of much shedding.

NAME	ZONE	HEIGHT IN FEET	FLOWERS, FRUITS, FOLIAGE	SHAPE AND CULTURE	REMARKS
Christmas Berry, see *Photinia*					
Cornus florida Flowering Dogwood	4–9	40	Large flat white or pink blooms in May; shiny red berries late summer to fall; crimson.	Branches spread laterally, but let low branches sweep ground. Needs shifting sun, deep watering in drought.	Handsome in every season; good companion for a hemlock.
Crab Apple, see *Malus*					
Crataegus laevigata (*oxyacantha*) English Hawthorn or May Tree	4–7	25	Fragrant, flat, snow-white blooms in May; red autumn fruits that hang into winter.	Thorny, rounded, low-branched tree or pruned high and open to see through. Sun or light shade; fast-growing.	Don't plant the thorny hawthorns near junipers, allow each a 15' spread.
C. phaenopyrum Washington Thorn	4–8	25	Clusters of mid-June cream-white flowers; fine red fruits cling into winter. Scarlet autumn coloring.	Rounded.	Native from Virginia to Alabama; heavy fruiting looks like a second blooming.
Dogwood, see *Cornus* English Hawthorn, see *Crataegus*					

Fringe Tree, see *Chionanthus*

Halesia carolina Silver-Bell or Snowdrop Tree	5–9	30	White bells strung along branches late Apr.–May ahead of leaves.	Can be pruned high to umbrella shape; grows well in sun or semi-shade, in acid soil.	Interesting seeds.
Ilex verticillata Black Alder or Winterberry	3–9	10	Brilliant red berries all along upper branches in clusters of three. Leaves blacken and fall in frost, but berries stay on until Mar.	A deciduous holly of swamps in the eastern and central states.	Likes acid soil and moisture. Good in cities. Male plants needed for pollination.
Magnolia soulangiana Saucer Magnolia	5–8	15	White to purple-pink flowers in Apr.–May; tree starts to bloom at 2'–3'; no fall coloring.	Interesting rounded form; gray bark. Best to transplant in spring.	Spectacular trees; need plenty of room.
Malus baccata Siberian Crab Apple	2–8	25	White, fragrant early May bloom; red and yellow fruits, favorite of summer birds.	Crab apples thrive in full sun in average soil. Pyramidal 'Columnaris' good for small places.	Early, extremely hardy. Oriental among most spectacular garden trees with shapely winter silhouette.

NAME	ZONE	HEIGHT IN FEET	FLOWERS, FRUITS, FOLIAGE	SHAPE AND CULTURE	REMARKS
M. floribunda Japanese Crab Apple	4–9	30	Pink, early May bloom. Late Aug. to mid-Oct. brings yellow and red fruits.	Rounded and densely branched.	Nice with a hemlock. 'Red Jade' grows to 20', has pendent red fruits lasting well into winter.
Maple, see *Acer* May Tree, see *Crataegus* Mountain Ash, see *Sorbus*					
Photinia villosa Christmas Berry	4–8	15	Small, white May flowers in flat clusters; red fruits favored by birds.	Shapely grower; needs sun.	Sun shining through clear amber autumn foliage a lovely sight. Choice small tree.
Prunus sargentii Japanese Cherry	4–8	40	Deep pink Apr.–May bloom; scarlet fall foliage.	Spreading, good specimen. Needs sun, rich, well-drained soil.	Upright 'Columnaris' good for small properties; water well in drought. Many other fine cultivars, upright and weeping.

P. subhirtella 'Pendula' Higan Cherry	5–8	25	Single pink flowers, small leaves.	Fine-textured look, graceful weeping form.	Very popular.
Redbud, see *Cercis* Rowan, see *Sorbus* Serviceberry, see *Amelanchier* Shadbush, see *Amelanchier* Silver-Bell Tree, see *Halesia*					
Sorbus aucuparia European Mountain Ash or Rowan	2–7	45	Clusters of white flowers in June. Brilliant orange-red fruit, much of which clings, despite robins, until early winter.	'Fastigiata', narrow upright; 'Pendula', weeping form.	Fine yellow-to-red autumn coloring.
Washington Thorn, see *Crataegus* Winterberry, see *Ilex*					

Echoing the vertical form of the adjacent chimney, a Japanese cedar, *Cryptomeria japonica*, makes a distinctive accent at the Julian C. Smith front door. Korean boxwood and mountain laurel are attractive throughout the year. *Bukovcik photo*

8

Evergreens, Glory of the Winter Garden

EVERGREENS ARE THE GLORY and the mainstay of the winter garden. Strategically placed, a tall pine, hemlock, or cryptomeria is an arresting accent; a group of mountain laurels softens the stern angles of a too-high foundation. A pair of dwarf Alberta spruce (*Picea glauca* 'Conica'), of Japanese yew, or of littleleaf (Korean) boxwood might offer a welcome beside your front steps. Although all are green, there are subtle differences of shade, as well as large differences in shape, among the evergreens. Half a century ago, a wise American gardener, Louise Beebe Wilder, wrote:

"Thus is the garden, well planted with evergreens, a cheerful and inviting place, even in the dead of winter . . . there is always something worth going to see. The impatient buds of the broad-leaved evergreens are worth watching—one feels they may open any day—and among the conifers there is rich colour: bronze and rust and mulberry, sea-green and gray and olive; the silvery bloom of the Junipers, the dusky tones of the Yews, the steadfast green of Laurel and Box. And in the 'noontide twilight' made by falling snow it is a delight to go among the evergreens and note the individual grace with which each bears its soft white burden. The Spruces carry it gaily, as if enjoying a winter sport; the Arborvitaes a trifle wearily, burdened by their finery; the Hemlocks proudly,

A tall American holly dominates a well-chosen evergreen entrance planting of Japanese holly, dwarf yew, and English ivy. An espaliered fire thorn against the house wall offers a pleasing form contrast to the Japanese holly. *Taloumis photo*

as queens once wore their jewels. . . . Snow drapes the Cedars in an ermine mantle, and clings about the spread branches of the hoary Pines as legends cling about the name."

Variety among the Evergreens

In today's smaller properties there is usually not enough room for more than one or two of the tall evergreens; grown perhaps in the far corners, these often make an appealing group with the different forms of a flowering tree

A tall and a dwarf yew with dwarf rhododendron and an edging of pachysandra make a green entrance planting that requires little care. *Genereux photo*

or a group of shrubs, especially those carrying winter fruits. (These are listed in the chart following Chapter 6.) I think of combining an upright hemlock with one flat-branched dogwood or with a Japanese maple or a weeping crab

Well-chosen evergreens of different heights—a tall Chinese juniper, medium-high Pfitzers, and spruces with clumps of boxwood—make a handsome and inviting doorway planting. Connecticut garden of Mr. and Mrs. Orville Prescott. *Owner photo*

apple, for example. A blue spruce is a beautiful companion for a star magnolia. The soft green of various kinds of chamaecyparis set off by a pink dogwood, the Chinese juniper 'Glauca', also a soft green, associated with a winter honeysuckle. The feathery silver-tipped argentea form of the false cypress is most effective standing alone. The gray-green Sargent juniper can cover your terrace like a rug.

As you consider your four-season garden, where evergreens will be of utmost importance, go to a nursery specializing in them; or if no suitable nursery is near you, study the excellent color photographs in the catalogue of Wayside Gardens (Hodges, S.C. 29695). Varietal names are so important. You can't just order a pine and expect to receive one you have admired at a neighbor's. The white pine is a giant that eventually reaches to 100 feet or more; the mugho pine reaches to only 4 feet.

The Cone-Bearers

It helps to think of this great evergreen clan as composed of large needle types like the pines, arborvitaes, cypresses, and hemlocks, and of small growers

ABOVE: In winter the awaiting buds of the broad-leaved mountain andromeda, *Pieris floribunda*, give the effect of a plant in bloom. *Taloumis photo.* BELOW: In January snow, the pink-blushed flower buds and the variegated evergreen foilage of the Japanese andromeda are a lovely sight. *Fitch photo*

The snow-covered leaves of the compact holly hybrid 'Blue Queen' look lovely in the winter garden. *Fitch photo*

like the Pfitzer junipers and spreading yews. All these are classified as cone-bearers or coniferous evergreens, although the cones of the last two look more like berries. Most of them require an acid soil and a sunny location. Only the yews and hemlocks, and to a lesser degree the arborvitaes, are shade-tolerant. Particularly recommended for small gardens are two slow-growing pines: the wide-spreading parasol Japanese, *Pinus densiflora* 'Umbraculifera', which grows slowly to 15 feet and is interesting for its open orange-bark trunk; and the compact Swiss stone pine, *P. cembra*, which is often columnar. If you want to save space but need narrow accents, consider such columnar types as *Juniperus chinensis, J. scopulorum*, and *J. virginiana*. Of course, the weeping forms of evergreens are outstandingly beautiful and are particularly effective when set alone in the winter garden, as the graceful drooping hemlock, *Tsuga canadensis* 'Pendula', and the blue Atlas cedar, *Cedrus atlantica* 'Pendula'.

Two Dwarf pines for small properties. LEFT: *Pinus mugo* 'Compacta'; RIGHT: the Swiss stone pine, *P. cembra* 'Nana', with pachysandra filling in below. *Taloumis photos*

Broad-leaved Evergreens

The broad-leaved evergreens are totally different plants and may be pleasing grouped by themselves or with a specimen conifer. The rhododendron is the best known, but this reacts so violently to cold weather that it is better omitted from the winter view. When you look at those tightly furled leaves on a cold day, you yourself are likely to have a chill. If you care for rhododendrons because of their flowers, try to plant them beyond your immediate winter view. But many other broad-leaved evergreens are essential for their effectiveness in the cold-weather months.

The holly is first and there are many hollies, tall trees like the handsome English and American ilexes, and dwarfs like the Japanese holly. The smaller

Two junipers of limited stature. ABOVE: The creeping 3-inch *J. squamata prostrata* provides a blue-green ground cover all year long. *Fitch photo*. BELOW: The Andorra juniper 'Plumosa' makes a pleasing in-scale accent beside a small pool. *Taloumis photo*

broad-leaved shrubs include andromeda, leucothoe, and my favorite, mountain laurel. Even in my small garden I have the first two and a lovely semicircle of laurel beyond the fence. The laurel can reach 10 feet, but slowly, and is beautiful in every season.

So many of the smaller broad-leaved evergreens have a great appeal, among them the various barberries, the littleleaf boxwood, the cranberry cotoneaster, and where there is sufficient shelter, the Japanese skimmia. Some of the azaleas may also prove evergreen for you as the Gables, Glen Dale, and Kurumi hybrids. In a protected corner of my fenced-in garden, a big Glen Dale holds on well.

If you now have broad-leaved evergreens that are scorched by winter sun and wind, you can protect them with a liquid latex spray. I have used one called Wilt-Pruf for years on the hardy candytuft border where it stretches into the sun. Two sprayings are required, one late in November and another late in February or early March. If you can procure the new Wilt-Pruf NCF, you will find that two sprayings in the fall, an hour apart, will be adequate, and you won't have to have that late-winter spray job on your mind. Work on a mild day when the temperature is in the 40s and is likely to remain so for twenty-four hours.

The charts in this chapter do not by any means present all the possibilities, but list concise information on what are generally considered to be the best plants in each category. Evergreen ground covers and evergreen ferns are also effective in the winter scene. Theirs are secondary values, emphasizing design and often contributing to the primary effects of tall or spreading evergreens.

Evergreen Ground Covers

In winter, areas of green coverage are a great asset in the garden. Some of the best of the ground covers are vinelike; others are low, upright growers. Their value may not be so noticeable in summer, but in the cold months their green stretches are a cheerful sight and when there is snow, a reassurance and excitement.

The upright Japanese spurge, *Pachysandra terminalis*, hardy in Zones 5 to 9, comfortable in sun or shade, and growing to 12 inches, is perhaps the ground cover most widely used. It covers an area quickly, so that you find yourself very soon able to offer quantities of plants to your neighbors. Bulbs grow nicely in the midst of pachysandra, particularly the very early 15-inch petticoat narcissus, *N. bulbocodium*, or the smaller *N. cyclameneus* variety 'February Gold'. These make a pretty picture late in winter.

A lustrous evergreen with spring-blooming flowers, myrtle—*Vinca minor*, also called periwinkle—is hardy in Zone 4 and far southward in sun or shade and makes a nice carpet for such early bulbs as the white form of glory-of-the-snow, *Chionodoxa luciliae*, or one of the yellow crocus species. Not only is myrtle dependable, but it is good for carpeting and valuable for defining beds; in this neat-edging role it needs considerable clipping.

English ivy, *Hedera helix*, hardy in Zones 5 to 9—I think the green is preferable to the variegated and extra-hardy Baltic type—grows slowly until established and must be planted where winter sunshine does not strike and brown it. It is excellent for all shaded areas, often naturalizing as it proceeds by small, rootlike holdfasts. A number of varieties are available but, for ground cover use, the type species is probably best, except in the coldest parts of Zone 5.

The wintercreeper, *Euonymus fortunei* 'Minima', hardy to Zones 5 to 8, has leaves less than ½ inch long. It is a slow grower but a most attractive ground cover. 'Vegeta' has somewhat larger, rounded, glossy leaves and is a good "rambler" with profuse orange-to-red fruits. This one is not so slow as is often claimed. It is more commonly used as a climber and may reach 8 feet in three years, as it has for me. I think 'Minima' is a better ground cover, or 'Kewensis' with the smallest leaves of them all. The golden-yellow winter aconites, the snowdrops, or green-tipped spring snowflakes look charming among euonymus foliage.

A great favorite of mine, too seldom seen, is the European ginger, *Asarum europaeum*. Hardy in Zone 4 and in the Appalachians southward, it has large, glossy, 2- to 3-inch kidney-shaped leaves on 5-inch stalks. It is best suited to the shade. Growing under a deciduous tree, such as a crab apple, or in a wide sweep along a walk, it is an arresting sight.

For certain locations the needled creeping junipers are ideal, although they are not "gardenesque" in the manner of these other four ground covers but have a shrubbery look. *Juniperus horizontalis* 'Wiltonii'—also offered as *J.* 'Blue Rug'—is an excellent *flat* grower for a terrace. It spreads a bluish haze over that part of my terrace in the sun; and where the plants come to the edge of the stonework, they grow gracefully over and down. Hardy in Zone 2 and southward, this does a beautiful covering job and has grown quickly for me.

The glossy evergreen leaves of the European ginger, *Asarum europaeum*, make an outstanding winter ground cover. *Fitch photo*

Sarcococca hookerana humilis is a charming plant if grown in groups of a dozen or so. Hardy in Zones 5 through 7, it has wiry stems from 1 to 3 feet high, with 3-inch-long evergreen leaves tapering at both ends, and in February to March inconspicuous fragrant flowers without petals but effective long stamens and pistil. It is related to Box.

The semievergreen bearberry cotoneaster, *C. horizontalis*, hardy from Zone 4 southward, is a shrubby grower, almost to 3 feet, particularly attractive where covering is wanted for a sunny or partially shaded wall or bank along a stream. It thrives in moist locations, and the long branches, often rooting as they grow, are studded with bright red berries. This cotoneaster is a pretty sight all winter.

Pachistima (or *Paxistima*) *canbyi,* a North American native, is an excellent evergreen of bronze winter hue to use as a ground cover in light shade, although in my experience it has been slow to spread. Hardy in Zones 5 to 8, and growing to 15 inches high, it makes a nice low hedge or a pleasing edging for taller evergreens, as in a foundation planting with various ericaceous plants, for pachistima also requires an acid soil.

An evergreen fern in two settings. ABOVE: The common *Polypodium vulgare* grows out of a warm rock crack. *Fitch photo.* BELOW: It spreads its beautiful wide form under a pine tree. *Taloumis photo*

A Scotch pine, *Pinus sylvestris*, the trunk overgrown with English ivy, is an effective accent for the Julian C. Smith garden, Westport, Conn. (plan on page 144). A mugho pine makes a pleasing accent in the corner of house and wall. *Bukovcik photo*

Evergreen Ferns

Of the evergreen ferns, three are well suited to planting among rocks and three others offer interesting variations among ground covers in the winter landscape. All of these are suitable for Zone 3 and appreciably farther south in shady, cool places.

In the rock garden the dense, creeping common polypody, *Polypodium vulgare*, is charming in light shade, on moderately dry leaf mold. Or let it cover a fallen log. It is delightful, with yellow-to-medium-green fronds, a cheerful stretch in the midst of the usual winter shades of brown.

The ebony spleenwort, *Asplenium platyneuron*, grows taller, to 20 inches. It likes a lightly shaded area in stony or sandy leaf mold. The narrow, dark green fronds form a crown, and a half-dozen plants together look like a little grove above the lower, creeping rock plants.

The purple cliff-brake, *Pellaea atropurpurea*, really a gray-green hue, grows 6 to 15 inches high in open shade, is native on limestone, and so grows best in slightly alkaline soil. The leathery tufted fronds are effective among rocks.

Familiar and delightful is the Christmas fern, *Polystichum acrostichoides*, which I plant between crocus or narcissus clumps for a dark green/bright yellow late-winter picture. This fern grows 15 to 30 inches tall in open shade in rich leaf mold and spreads slowly.

Then there are two shield or wood ferns to consider. They will grow from northern Zone 3, where they are green for at least the early part of the winter, and down into Zone 7 and the cooler areas of Zone 8. The deep green *Dryopteris austriaca intermedia* may reach 30 inches and so looks best planted in a wide sweep. It thrives in moist, humusy soil, in partial shade. The deeply cut, dark green, prickly fronds make a crisp and effective cold-weather picture.

The leathery blue-green wood fern, *D. marginalis,* is not so tall, to 20 inches, and grows in vase form. It is fine as an accent plant or for a broad green stretch in shady woodland.

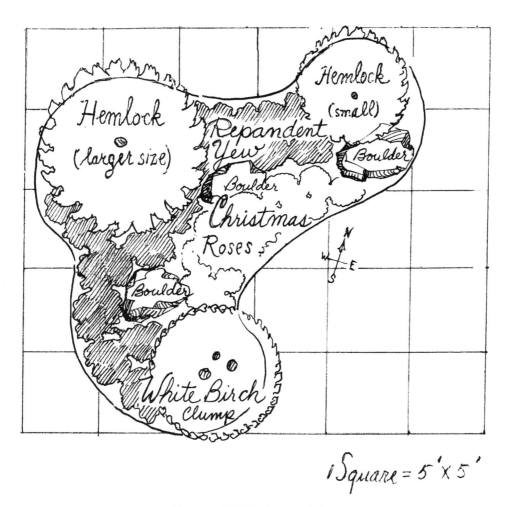

Square = 5' x 5'

Green-and-White Winter Effect

Hemlock (*Tsuga canadensis* or *T. caroliniana*, or both).
White birch (*Betula papyrifera*).
Christmas roses (*Helleborus niger*).
Repandent yew (*Taxus baccata* 'Repandens') as ground cover.
Snowdrops and Christmas ferns can be grown beneath the birch.

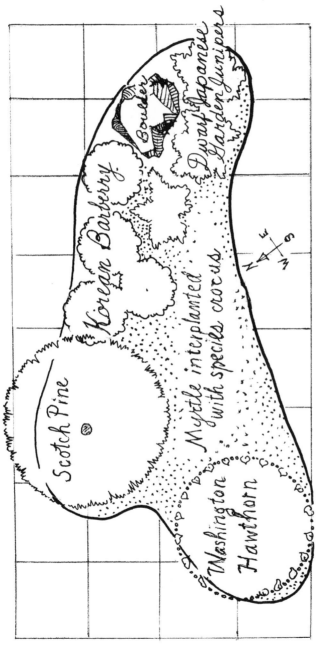

1 Square = 5' x 5'

Evergreens and Red Berries

Scotch pine (*Pinus sylvestris*); bluish needles and coppery bark.

Washington thorn (*Crataegus phaenopyrum*); long-lasting scarlet berries contrast and harmonize with colors of pine

Korean barberry (*Berberis koreana*); pendent clusters of red fruit; deciduous but dense, twiggy branches.

Dwarf Japanese garden juniper (*Juniperus procumbens* 'Nana'); its low, bluish-green foliage echoes that of the pine.

Myrtle (*Vinca minor*) makes a low, dark green foreground and ties the whole scheme together.

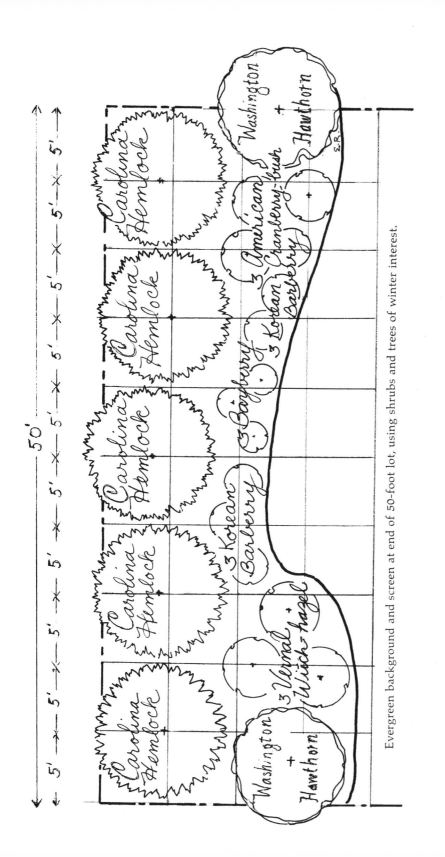

Evergreen background and screen at end of 50-foot lot, using shrubs and trees of winter interest.

Labels within the figure:

50'
5' — 5' — 5' — 5' — 5' — 5' — 5' — 5' — 5' — 5'

Carolina Hemlock
Carolina Hemlock
Carolina Hemlock
Carolina Hemlock
Carolina Hemlock

Washington + Hawthorn
Washington + Hawthorn

3 American Cranberry-bush
3 Korean Barberry
3 Bayberry
3 Korean Barberry
3 Vernal Witch-hazel

S.R.

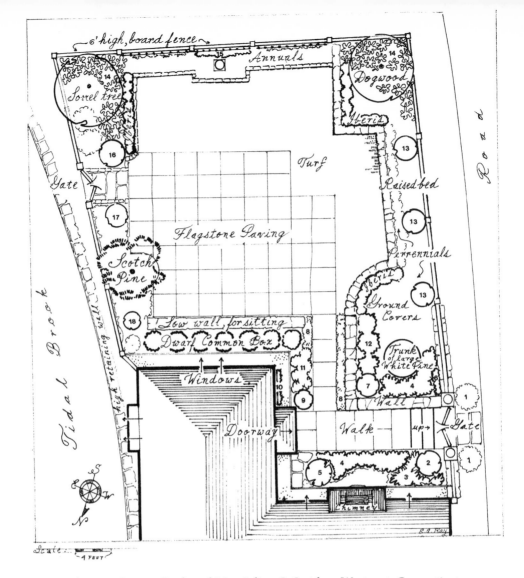

The Four-Season Garden of Mrs. Julian C. Smith at Westport, Connecticut
Designed by Eloise A. Ray, L.A.

1 Brown's Yew (*Taxus media* 'Brownii')
2 Littleleaf Japanese Holly (*Ilex crenata*)
3 Christmas Rose (*Helleborus niger*)
4 European Wild Ginger (*Asarum europaeum*)
5 Cherry Laurel (*Prunus laurocerasus*)
6 Purpleleaf Wintercreeper (*Euonymus fortunei* 'Colorata')
7 'Emerald Isle' (*Euonymus fortunei* 'Emerald Isle')
8 Partridgeberry (*Mitchella repens*)
9 English Yew (*Taxus baccata* 'Adpressa')
10 Hatfield Yew, espaliered (*Taxus media* 'Hatfieldii')
11 Mountain Cranberry (*Vaccinium vitis-idaea minus*)
12 Leucothoe (*Leucothoe fontanesiana* or *catesbaei*)
13 Azalea 'Ruth May' (*Rhododendron* hybrid)
14 Christmas Fern (*Polystichum acrostichoides*)
15 Miniature Wintercreeper (*Euonymus fortunei* 'Minima')
16 Spreading Euonymus, upright shrub (*Euonymus kiautschovica* or *E. patens*)
17 Mugho Pine (*Pinus mugo mugo*)
18 'Silver Queen' (*Euonymus fortunei* 'Variegata')

Large Distinctive Evergreens for Accent or Screen

These conifers (cone-bearers) are all handsome trees to be used discreetly on smaller properties, but a specimen pine or hemlock is essential for every winter garden.

NAME	ZONE	HEIGHT IN FEET	GROWTH	SHAPE	REMARKS
Abies concolor White or Colorado Fir	3–6	100	Medium to slow.	Dense and pyramidal; finely textured, blue-green needles. All firs good specimens where room.	Upright 3″ tapered cones; don't prune off lower branches, not renewable. Full sun.
Cedar, see *Cedrus*					
Cedrus atlantica 'Glauca' Atlas Cedar	6–9	100	Fast.	Narrow then widely pyramidal; silvery, light green effect. 'Pendula', graceful drooping form.	Both cedars handsome. Develop flat tops with age (not same as pointed red cedar, *Juniperus virginiana*). Both do well near the sea.
C. libani Cedar-of-Lebanon	6–9	100	Slow.		
Chamaecyparis obtusa Hinoki False Cypress	4–8	120	Slow.	Broadly pyramidal, dark and glossy.	Excellent specimen for a big place, also good for screening.

NAME	ZONE	HEIGHT IN FEET	GROWTH	SHAPE	REMARKS
Cryptomeria japonica Japanese Cedar	5–9	125	Fast.	Irregularly pyramidal with tiny rounded cones. Bronze winter tone.	Individual, elegant; for formal rather than country place; develops enormous girth; requires protection from sun and wind.
False Cypress, see *Chamaecyparis* Fir, see *Abies* Hemlock, see *Tsuga* Japanese Cedar, see *Cryptomeria*					
Picea abies Norway Spruce	2–7	125	Fast.	Cone-shaped.	Most widely grown evergreen in U.S., but can be disappointing in maturity. Has very dark needles; there is a graceful pendulous form. Many dwarf forms, which see.
P. glauca Alberta Spruce	2–6	80	Slow.	Compact shape and very hardy. Small branches drooping.	'Densata', Black Hills Spruce, slow-growing, to 20'; blue-green needles.

P. omorika Serbian Spruce	4–7	100	Medium.	Narrow.	Excellent tree; glossy green, flat needles. 'Pendula' a beautiful form with curving branches.
P. pungens Colorado Spruce	2–8	100	Slow.	Broad pyramid.	Long popular, extremely well known, and hardy, but tends to lose its special character when mature. Also a weeping form.

Pine, see *Pinus*

Pinus bungeana Lace-Bark Pine	4–6	75	Slow.	Spreading; several trunks.	Unusual Chinese tree quite hardy to Mass. Dark green needles, exfoliating bark in decorative patterns.
P. cembra Swiss Stone Pine	2–6	75	Slow.	Stiff, pyramidal; dark blue-green effect.	Very hardy, rather like *P. strobus* but of less open growth and the branches are less horizontal.

NAME	ZONE	HEIGHT IN FEET	GROWTH	SHAPE	REMARKS
P. densiflora 'Umbraculifera' Japanese Umbrella Pine	4–8	15	Slow.	Wide-spreading, fan-shaped with many trunks.	Picturesque; the branchlets have orange-yellow bark. Needs space; handsome specimen.
P. nigra Austrian Pine	3–8	100	Fast.	Pyramidal, may have flat top in age; stiff, dark needles.	Strong and handsome as a specimen, for mass screening, or for formal hedge; 4″ to 6″ cones. Plant all pines in full sun.
P. strobus White Pine	3–7	120	Fast.	Tall, broad, pyramidal; finely textured; soft and dense.	A native with large cones; transplants easily; excellent screen. Lovely in all seasons, but not for South.
P. thunbergi Japanese Black Pine	3–8	100	Fast.	Irregular, open, interesting form.	Best evergreen for seashore, even close to water, endures salt-water spray; not for inland; 3″ or smaller cones.

Spruce, see *Picea*

Tsuga canadensis Canadian Hemlock	3–7	90	Fast.	Shade-tolerant; shapely, graceful pyramid; feathery, long-lived; can be clipped as a tall hedge.	Native, among loveliest of evergreens as specimen or screen. ('Pendula', the Sargent hemlock, is flat on top, grows up to 4' in height but up to 50' across.)
T. caroliniana Carolina Hemlock	4–7	70	Fast.	Most graceful; slender, densely needled branches full of light and shadow.	"Absolutely hardy, with rich blackgreen leaves, silvery below, this tree is ever a picture fascinating and charming." —E. H. Wilson

Needle Evergreens for Small Places

Many nurseries and nursery catalogues today include a great number of these useful needle evergreens, most of which do not grow tall but broad.

NAME	ZONE	HEIGHT IN FEET	FORM	CULTURE	REMARKS
Hemlock, see *Tsuga*					
Juniperus chinensis 'Sargentii' Sargent Juniper	2–9	1	Spreading 8' to 10' in maturity. Fine gray-green ground cover.	All junipers need sun, tolerate poor soil, even drought.	Junipers among hardiest of evergreens.
J. horizontalis 'Douglasii' Waukegan Juniper	2–9	1	Low, trailing form.		Steel-blue cast toward purple in winter. Good ground cover.
J. h. 'Emerson'		1	Very slow-growing.		Prostrate. Blue all winter.
J. h. 'Plumosa' Andorra Juniper		1½	Low, ascending branches, spreading to 6' or more.		Prune regularly to avoid legginess and let light into lowest branches. Bronze in fall; purple in winter.
J. h. 'Wiltonii' or Blue Rug		1½	Flat, excellent ground cover.		Pleasing color for terrace.

Name	Zones	Height	Form	Remarks
J. procumbens 'Nana' Japanese Garden Juniper	4–8	2	Low and spreading with "shelved" branches.	Bluish-green needles; excellent, rounded dwarf form. Best of smaller kinds.
J. sabina 'Tamariscifolia' Tamarix Juniper	3–9	6	Fast-growing, spreading and mounded.	Feathery light green; endures city pollution; considered "best variety."
J. virginiana 'Canaertii' Red Cedar	2–9	12	Compact pyramidal form. Taller than other junipers but narrow plant. Female plant.	Dense rich green. Showy bluish fruits. Avoid near apple trees. Nice for a meadow.
Picea abies 'Clanbrasiliana' Dwarf Norway Spruce	3–7	7	Dense, flat-topped mound.	Dwarf spruces need sun and drained, not heavy, soil and should not be crowded. They are rather slow-growing.	Glossy green, with whitish branchlets.
P. a. 'Maxwellii' Maxwell Spruce	3–7	2	Twice as broad as high.	Needles leaf-green with hairlike tips.
P. a. 'Nidiformis'	3–7	2	Flat nest shape.	No other evergreen has quite this form.

NAME	ZONE	HEIGHT IN FEET	FORM	CULTURE	REMARKS
P. glauca 'Conica' Dwarf Alberta Spruce	3–7	6	Compact cone.		Bright grass-green needles.
P. g. 'Densata' Black Hills Spruce	3–7	8	Broad cone.		If not pruned, will eventually reach to 25' or more. Makes a fine hedge or windbreak.
P. pungens 'Bakeri' Colorado Spruce variety	3–7	8	Pyramidal.		The bluest of all spruces.
Pine, see *Pinus*					
Pinus cembra 'Nana' Swiss Stone Pine	2–6	3	Tightly pyramidal.	Needs sun, tolerates wind.	Hardy, very slow-growing; foliage same color as white pine. Cones 3½"; edible seeds for birds.
P. mugo 'Compacta' Mugho or Swiss Mountain Pine	2–7	4	Rounded and shiny.		Hardy, grows slowly when young; good for doorways, foundations; needs some pruning to keep small and shapely; 2" cones.

P. m. 'Pumila' Dwarf Stone Pine	2–7	½	Tiny and spreading.	A bristling cushion.
Red Cedar, see *Juniperus virginiana* Spruce, see *Picea*				
Taxus baccata 'Repandens' English Yew	6–8	4	Nearly prostrate; leaves blue-green. Flat-topped with pendulous branch tips.	Hardiest of English varieties and fruiting; not so hardy as *I. cuspidata*.
				All yews thrive in sun and tolerate shade, even north side of house.
T. cuspidata 'Densa' Dwarf Japanese Yew	4–8	4	15' or more across.	Very hardy. Try to select female plants with attractive red berries.
T. c. 'Nana'	4–8	8	20' across.	Judicious pruning keeps it low; no shearing necessary.
T. media 'Hatfieldii' Hatfield Yew	3–7	10	Broad, columnar, 10' across.	For corners of house, not beside front door.
T. m. 'Hicksii'	3–7	6	Narrow, columnar.	Excellent for hedge.
Tsuga canadensis 'Pendula' Sargent Hemlock	4–7	4	Flat-topped, dense; very prostrate; long-lived.	Fascinating knee-high expanse of densely green, low-arching branches.
Yew, see *Taxus*				

Broad-leaved Shrubs and Trees for Winter Effect

These are among the most beautiful of the shrubs and trees for winter. Be sure to note heights.

NAME	ZONE	HEIGHT IN FEET	FLOWERS, FRUIT, FOLIAGE	CULTURE	REMARKS
Andromeda, see *Pieris* Barberry, see *Berberis*					
Berberis julianae Wintergreen Barberry	5–9	5	Yellow flowers; blue-black fruit.	Sun.	Barberries make good spiny hedge plants that need no trimming.
B. mentorensis	4–7	3	Dull red fruits; strong dark green leaves.		Semievergreen, stands more heat and drought than most. Good hedge.
B. triacanthophora (now *wisleyensis*) Three Spine Barberry	5–8	3	Blue-black fruit.		Evergreen, very thorny.
B. verruculosa Warty Barberry	5–8	3	Dark purplish fruit; shiny green, leathery leaves, white below.		One of the best of the evergreen barberries; bronze winter foliage.
Boxwood, see *Buxus*					

Name	Zones	Height	Description	Light	Remarks
Buxus microphylla koreana Littleleaf or Korean Boxwood	4–7	3	Excellent foliage.	Shade.	Useful for low hedge; hardier than English. Avoid winter wind as leaves may brown. See newer cultivars as 'Tide Hill' or 'Wintergreen', which more dependably do not brown.
B. sempervirens Tree Boxwood	5–9	20			Marvelous hedge or accent plant; slow-growing, may be sheared or not.
B. s. 'Suffruticosa'	5–9	½			Fine for edging; slow-growing.
Calluna vulgaris Heather	4–6	3	Very small white-to-purple summer flowers. Bronze winter leaf color.	Sun or shade; do not let dry out in drought. Needs cold weather and snow.	
Cotoneaster dammeri Bearberry Cotoneaster	5–8	1	Bright red fruits on long branches; fine ground cover.	Sun or shade.	Excellent evergreen for moist soil; may root along branches.

NAME	ZONE	HEIGHT IN FEET	FLOWERS, FRUIT, FOLIAGE	CULTURE	REMARKS
C. horizontalis Rockspray	4–8	3	Red fruits, semi-evergreen leaves on upper side of horizontal branches.	Sun or shade.	Excellent specimen or ground cover; most popular cotoneaster. Valuable for horizontal growth; attractive in a rock garden, grown over a wall, or espaliered.
C. microphylla Small-leaved Cotoneaster	3–9	3	Shining leaves, scarlet berries.		Excellent to plant prominently; gorgeous red winter mound, fruit hanging into winter.
Heather, see *Calluna* Holly, see *Ilex*					
Ilex aquifolium English Holly	6–7	40	Handsome tree where hardy; plants vary. Set out in spring.	Sun or light shade.	Protect from winter sun but summer sun desirable. North side of buildings or of other evergreens is a good location.

I. cornuta Chinese Holly	6–9	9–10	Bright red berries through winter; dark green shining leaves.	Slow-growing. Also form with yellow fruits. May expire under temperatures below 10 degrees F. But some fine specimens about 4' high in a N.Y. City garden survived at 0 degrees F. 'Burfordii' is hardiest clone.
I. crenata Japanese Holly *I. c.* 'Helleri' *I. c.* 'Microphylla' *I. c.* 'Stokes'	5–8	15	Beautiful small-leaved, mounded growth.	Species excellent, fast-growing, undemanding; nice for doorways or with small flowering trees; can be pruned to 5'; cultivars, dwarf and compact, to 4'.
I. glabra Inkberry	3–9	10	Black berries. Dark green lustrous leaves; fine shrub.	Native; can be grown in swampy areas.
I. opaca American Holly	5–9	50	Red berries on dark green leaves. Hardy and fast-growing.	Beautiful native; give important placement; both male and female plants necessary for fruiting.

NAME	ZONE	HEIGHT IN FEET	FLOWERS, FRUIT, FOLIAGE	CULTURE	REMARKS
Inkberry, see *Ilex*					
Kalmia latifolia Mountain Laurel	4–8	10	June, pink-white shell-like flowers, also deeper-pink-to-red clones.	Sun or semishade.	Easy to keep low by pruning; one of the very best; native American plant. True laurel a Mediterranean plant.
Leucothoe catesbaei (now *L. fontanesiana*) Drooping Leucothoe	5–8	6	Apr.–May.	Stands heavy shade. Acid soil.	Small graceful shrub; good in association with andromeda and mountain laurel.
Mahonia aquifolium Oregon Holly Grape	5–8	4	Fragrant chartreuse flowers in May; blue summer fruits.	Sun or part shade.	Can be rampant, traveling far by underground runners; stands hard pruning.
M. bealei Leatherleaf Mahonia	6–9	8	Fragrant yellow flowers, blue fruit, hollylike leaflets.	Part shade, tolerates lime.	Excellent for foundation planting; protect from winter sun and wind; prune as desired.
Mountain Laurel, see *Kalmia* Oregon Holly Grape, see *Mahonia*					

Pieris floribunda Mountain Andromeda	4–8	6	Upright, white pyramidal clusters.	Semishade.	Hardy, fine for on-view plantings out of the sun. Clone 'Dorothy Wycoff' has leaves touched with red in winter.
P. japonica Japanese Andromeda or Lily-of-the-Valley Bush	5–9	9	Drooping, fragrant flowers in mid-Apr., just before P. floribunda.		
Pyracantha coccinea 'Lalandei' Laland Fire Thorn	5–9	15	White flowers in large clusters in May; spectacular orange berries in fall.	Sun.	Attractive against a wall or tied to a trellis.
Sarcococca hookerana humilis Sweet Box	5–7	1–3	Tapering 3″ leaves on wiry stems. Inconspicuous fragrant flowers Feb.–Mar.		Charming ground cover, goes well with Leucothoe.
Skimmia japonica Japanese Skimmia	7–8	5	White spring blooms, then red fruit. (S. 'Reevesiana' has perfect flowers, so every plant is fruitful.)	Part shade.	Male and female plants both necessary for bloom; needs sheltered location to survive north of Philadelphia. Small size makes it useful.

159

Light from a pole lantern, controlled by an electric timer in the house, makes my garden glow in dusk. *Swinehart photo*

9

Lights to Extend Your Garden Pleasure

UNTIL YOU HAVE ACHIEVED a fine night picture—or more than one—in your garden, you cannot imagine what great pleasure you are missing, for the dead of winter, lighted, is indeed a lovely sight. For a small place, like my present garden, one lantern light supported on a 6-foot pole gives charming winter pictures, especially when there is snow. Both lantern and pole came from an electric supplier. The electrician who wired them provided an automatic timer, which in winter is set for the end of dusk, 4:30 P.M., to make the garden glow just as the sun goes down. The light goes off at 11:00 P.M., too late for me to enjoy garden views, lighted or otherwise. Because mine is a garden of formal design, the night lighting emphasizes all sorts of interesting shadowed angles, and these, of course, can be best appreciated from the living-room windows and the glassed-in plant alcove. Beyond the fence, one great pine is a handsome sight, but the framework of the white birch silhouetted against the dark green of the hemlocks is loveliest of all—a magic picture.

When I had a larger area to light, I came upon the dark winter views quite by accident. Having installed some high house-corner "burglar" lights for practical rather than aesthetic reasons, I discovered one snowy evening as I looked out from the darkened house that my white birch clump at the kitchen window was

A suspended lantern on a post is one of many garden lights now available. Night beauty, especially in snow, is marvelously enhanced by good lighting. *Taloumis photo*

To illuminate their small garden and the hedge of dwarf yews that runs along the terrace, my neighbors, the Eugene Reeds, installed a row of these small standards, wired to an outdoor switch. *Swinehart photo*

162

By day or night, a well-designed
lantern like this is an attractive addition to the garden. *Fitch photo*

an exquisite sight. I decided then to work out panoramas for other windows, and
to start at once, even though it was January and there was snow.

In carrying out my plans—and you must allow plenty of time for consideration
of lighting effects—I had the assistance of my very patient contractor. He waded
back and forth through snow on the lawn and the cliff-side of the brook until
we found what we thought was the just-right placement and angle for lights.
But in spring they were moved again to the house side of the brook. Experiment
was easily managed with temporary lights on a 200-foot extension cord plugged
into an outside outlet on the terrace. There they stayed all winter while I made
up my mind. Eventually an indoor control switch was installed.

You will find that such experiment is helpful in selecting your favorite view,
or views—the tree or garden or landscape area you wish to light for evening
enjoyment. You want to discover what is worth lighting, to find out from what
windows or doors of your house you are most likely to get pleasure from night
pictures. Of course, you want to avoid overdoing; the effect you desire is
ethereal, not amusement-park exciting.

My neighbors light their little garden and dwarf yew hedge with a row of 30-inch standard lanterns. These illuminate an area rather than spotlight a specimen tree or shrub. The standards are easy to install, a matter of connecting the wire of each one to a main outdoor cord plugged into a terrace outlet. The trench for this type of wiring needs to be only 3 to 4 inches deep. These standards are but one of a number of outdoor lights now available at well-stocked hardware stores or shops specializing in electrical equipment.

Of course, there are various other ways to light a garden area or favorite tree or perhaps a group of trees next to a rock. Cords can be strung out from the house and through a tree, a floodlight fastened to a branch. Burglar lights along eaves or at house corners on the ground or high up can also serve to light a winter garden picture if you direct them strategically. At Christmas you may want to feature your doorway decoration or dramatize one great holly tree or pine. Your electrician can help you work out any of these plans once you know what you want. My point is that outdoor lighting is neither complicated nor costly—and the resulting winter garden picture is delightful beyond your dreams.

Your final view of what I see from my west window—my ceramic squirrel set on a section of log with the trunk of the white birch at one side and mountain laurel for a background. *Swinehart photo*

Where to Buy

Alpenglow Gardens, 13328 King George Highway, North Surrey, B.C., Canada. Dwarf conifers; catalogue 25¢.

Brimfield Gardens Nursery, 245 Brimfield Rd., Wethersfield, Conn. 06109. Trees, shrubs, ground covers; catalogue 25¢.

Carroll Gardens, Westminster, Md. 21157. Hellebores, ground covers, shrubs, dwarf evergreens.

P. de Jager & Sons, South Hamilton, Mass. 01982. Bulbs.

Dutch Mountain Nursery, Route 1, Box 67, Augusta, Mich. 49012. Trees, shrubs; plants for birds and conservation.

Garden Place, 6780 Heisley Rd., Mentor, Ohio 44060. Hellebores.

Girard Nurseries, Geneva, Ohio 44041. Trees and shrubs; azaleas.

Hyde's Inc., 56 Felton St. (Box 168), Waltham, Mass. 02154. Bird-feeders and bird-houses.

Lamb Nurseries, E. 101 Sharp Ave., Spokane, Wash. 99202. Hellebores, shrubs, ground covers.

Mayfair Nurseries, R.D. 2, Nichols, N.Y. 13812. Trees and shrubs; dwarf conifers, ground covers; catalogue 25¢.

Satellite Corp., Box 78, Manhasset, N.Y. 11030. Bird-feeders and birdhouses.

The Tingle Nursery Co., Pittsville, Md. 21850. Trees, shrubs, azaleas, hollies.

Upper Bank Nurseries, Inc., Media, Pa. 19000. Shrubs, trees, evergreens.

Van Bourgondien Brothers, 245 Farmingdale Rd., Box A, Babylon, N.Y. 11702. Bulbs.

Wayside Gardens, Hodges, S.C. 29695. General, with wide selection of fine varieties; handsome color catalogue $2, refundable with order.

White Flower Farm, Litchfield, Conn. 06759. General selection and excellent *Garden Book* with good cultural advice; catalogue $2, refundable with order.

Index

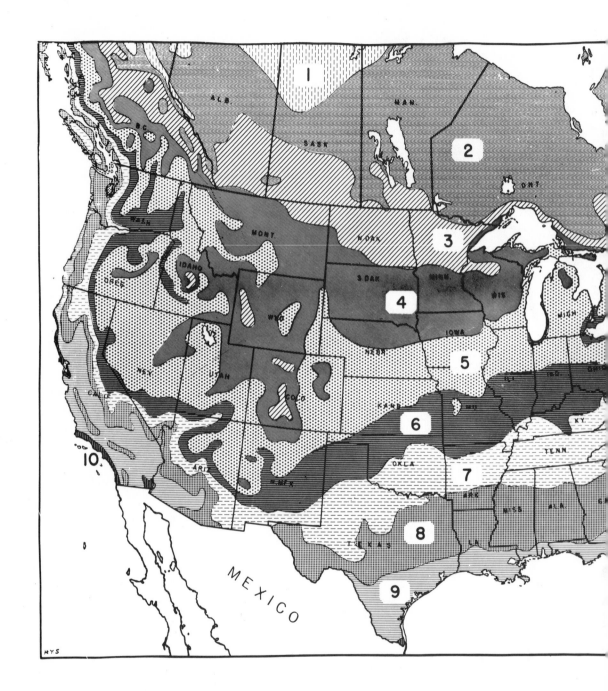